STUDIES IN CONTRACTUAL CLAIMS 12

CONTRACTORS' CLAIMS UNDER THE JCT INTERMEDIATE FORM OF CONTRACT

By R. D. Wood
FRICS, FCIOB, FCIArb, FInstD
Chartered Quantity Surveyor
Chartered Builder

CHARTERED INSTITUTE OF BUILDING, ENGLEMERE, KINGS RIDE, ASCOT, BERKSHIRE SL5 8BJ

FOREWORD

In writing on the Joint Contracts Tribunal's (JCT) Intermediate Form of Building Contract (IFC 84) - 1984 edition incorporating amendments 1:1986, 2:1987, 3:1988, 4:1988 and 5:1988, the views expressed are my own and not necessarily those of The Chartered Institute of Building (CIOB).

In general, the contract is examined from the standpoint of the Contractor. In doing so, I have attempted to follow the postulate of Lord Diplock in the case of *Miramar Maritime Corporation v Holborn Oil Trading* (1984)(HOL): '*Commercial documents and contracts should be construed in a manner which makes good commercial sense and not by a detailed semantic and syntactical analysis that would defeat the commercial purpose of the document or contract.*' I also have stressed the legal/technical relationship of the contract as it is here that I believe success can be obtained.

The Intermediate Form of Contract, whilst stating on its cover that it is for works of simple contract, is in itself very complicated.

In view of the contractual complexities of Named Sub-contractors (ie non-nominated specialists), the commentary is restricted in this publication to those contractual claims by the Main Contractor against the Employer. Similarly, the very complicated and far-ranging problems arising from all risks insurance have not been considered.

There are now at least two Standard Methods of Measurement which may be used in the preparation of the contract bills and equal reference is made in the text to both the 6th and the 7th editions.

It is important to appreciate that there still continues to be a considerable degree of litigation concerning the various standard forms of contracts issued by the JCT, with their many amendments and changes.

In consequence, it follows that there is a very real need for the Contractor to up-date continuously the legal interpretation of these contracts. Cases can progress from the High Court to the Court of Appeal and even up to the House of Lords. In the case of *Scottish Special Housing Association v Wimpey Construction (UK) Ltd (1986)* the two lower courts took one opinion whereas the House of Lords took the entirely opposite view. The annual publication *Contracts and Building Law Review,* published by the CIOB, provides a valuable reference for updating purposes.

Further, it is necessary to be aware of the JCT policy in updating its various forms of contract on a regular basis.

The Contractor would also be well advised to make reference to JCT Practice Note No. 20, which gives guidance on the choice of the appropriate form of contract, as well Practice Note IH/1, which provides an introduction to the Intermediate Form of Contract itself.

R. D. Wood
August 1991

ACKNOWLEDGEMENTS

The clauses of the JCT Intermediate Standard Form of Building Contract (1984) and amendments are reproduced by the kind permission of RIBA Publications Ltd., the copyright holder.

Permission to quote from the 6th and 7th editions of the Standard Method of Measurement is given by kind permission of the Royal Institution of Chartered Surveyors and the Building Employers' Confederation.

For permission to reproduce from the All England Law Reports of 1990 ALL ERI - (Part 8) - page 512 - the case of *William v Roffrey Brothers and Nicholls (Contractors) Ltd,* grateful thanks are also given to Butterworths Law Publishers, London.

CONTENTS

List of Figures and Tables

GLOSSARY

fait accompli = a thing already done or accomplished fact or not worth arguing about

functus officio = discharge of duty

force majeure = irresistible force

vis major = irresistible force

quantum meruit = reasonable payment

restituto in integrem = restoration to original position

quasi ex-contractu = implied from a contract

obligatio quasi ex-contra = obligation implied from a contract

ad em = the same

mutatis mutandis = the necessary changes being made

inter alia = between other things

contra proferentum = against the person drafting a contract

simpliciter = absolutely, universally or without limitation

1. Introduction

Basis of claims

Under the Intermediate Form of Building Contract (1988) a contractual claim is defined as: *'a legally justified demand or the assertion of a right from the Contractor for prolongation, disruption, dislocation and other direct loss and/or expense incurred by the Contractor due to issued instructions, default by the Employer or his Architect or other agents as provided for in specific contract clauses.'* These are defined contractual claims because they arise specifically from a clause in the contract, as for instance clause 4.11. However, there are claims that can be made by a Contractor by reason of breaches of contract brought about by the Employer, his Architect or any other agents of the Employer employed under the contract, such as an electrical, mechanical, structural or lift engineer. Such breaches of contract are dealt with under the final paragraph of clause 4.11.

Similarly, breaches of warranty are dealt with under the same clause and certain breaches of contract allow the Contractor to determine his own employment under the contract. (See clauses 7.5., 7.6., 7.7., 7.8. and 7.9.) Generally, breaches of contract (if allowed to continue) are believed to be sufficiently serious as to allow the Contractor to repudiate the contract. On the other hand, breaches of warranty are generally of a nature only to allow the Contractor damages. A very serious breach of contract could possibly involve rescission. Rescission is the total rejection of a contract by the Contractor because the Employer, by his conduct, clearly demonstrates that he does not intend to continue to be bound with the contract.

Rescission is preferable legally to repudiation because repudiation is only available for a breach of contract which goes to the very root of a contract, whilst rescission extends to a wider scope of rejection of a contract.

Note the discussion of 'repudiation' in the legal judgments of *Federal Commerce v Molena* (1979) (AC757 & 779) (Hol) and *Photo Production Ltd v Securicor Transport Ltd* (1980) (AC827 & 849) (Hol).

The Employer's Architect and Quantity Surveyor are not empowered under the contract to deal with breaches of contract not covered by contractual claim clauses.

Whilst some breaches of contract are clearly covered by specific clauses in the contract, it will be clearly seen that there are breaches of contract not covered. If there is any doubt on the part of the Contractor he must seek early advice as to the precise contractual solution from a specialist adviser. Claims arising from breaches of contract not covered by contractual claim clauses are often referred to as 'obligatio quasi ex contractu claims'.

This publication is limited solely to those claims which arise out of claim clauses of the contract.

It is always sound advice to avoid exaggerating the financial value of a claim, as this may well be self-defeating in the long run. It is far better for the Contractor to limit himself to a realistic loss and/or expense claim than to exaggerate the claim and incur considerable additional expense in obtaining external 'expert' advice.

The circumstances would be different if the Contractor decides to go to litigation or arbitration where, should he be successful, some portion of the costs (but by no means all) may be recouped from the Employer.

Ex-gratia claims

It is understandable, but regrettable, that some Contractors believe that they can rely on ex gratia or sympathetic claims. However, such claims do not have any legal derivation, neither are they breaches of contract or warranty. If they were then they would have been pursued as such legal matters. Ex gratia claims usually relate to those matters which have arisen out of hardship or misfortune but which are not due to the action of the Employer or his agents.

Therefore, the Employer is under no legal obligation whatsoever to meet any of these financial claims. Only rarely may he feel that the Contractor might be offered some consideration out of equity, common sense or sympathy. There are examples of ex gratia claims made by central and local government in the past. Following the oil crisis in the Middle East, when the price of oil quadrupled very swiftly, Contractors were offered 90% of their additional expenditure on fuel provided their contract was in a loss situation but not if they were certain to go into liquidation.

A second example concerned the enactment of Selective Employment Tax. Here, Contractors were offered 90% of the total value of this tax, provided their contract was in being at the time of its imposition.

The final example concerns the very considerable price increases during the period 1972 - 1975 where Contractors on fixed price contracts were being driven into liquidation. It was obviously prudent for the Employer to go some way towards ameliorating the losses caused by inflation. For a Contractor to go into liquidation can cause considerable additional expense to the Employer and doubtless this had been borne in mind when agreeing to an ex gratia claim.

Fundamental claims

On the majority of building contracts there are two fundamental types of claim:

Claims relating to time
A claim for an extension of time is sought because circumstances prevent the contract period being met. Providing the delay is not caused by the Contractor but by the Employer, the Architect, or any other agents of the Employer or by any of the events given in clause 2.4., an extension of time may be granted by the Architect. The Contractor also avoids paying liquidated and ascertained damages for the period of the extension of time granted.

Claims relating to money
These claims may be limited to:
(a) prolongation of Preliminaries;

(b) disruption, dislocation and disturbance;

(c) additional plant;

(d) additional site staff as well as supervising personnel;

(e) extra visits to site for specialist sub-contractor such as an asphalter;

(f) effect of new materials to the contract due to variations;

(g) effect of the alteration or modification of the design or quality or quantity of the works by virtue of variations under clause 3.6.

A detailed examination of some claims and their grounds will be considered later.

2. JCT Intermediate Form of Building Contract (incorporating Amendments 1 to 5)

Throughout this publication, the abbreviation IFC84 will be used to denote the JCT Intermediate Form of Contract.

It would seem that the IFC84 lies financially between the JCT Agreement for Minor Works and the JCT 80 standard form of building contract (JCT80), ie more detailed than the Minor Works Agreement and less detailed than JCT 80 but with distinctly new legal issues of its own, such as clause 2.8. - the repayment of liquidated damages or clause 3.13.1. - Architect's instructions concerning the failure of work. The deletion of certain clauses is effected by means of the appendix and alternatives are similarly possible for clauses 2.4.10. or 6.3.1., which is a distinct improvement over some other standard forms of building contract. The JCT has stated that it is intended to make further amendments from time to time and, therefore, it will become absolutely fundamental for a Contractor to check and see if any contract he is tendering for has any additional clauses and changes from the standard form.

A thorough grasp of contract law, common law, statute law and a full understanding of IFC84 and all its internal implications, as well as the legal remedies which are available to the Contractor, is needed in order to bring to light or detect whether there are any contractual claims on a specific contract. This, in turn, will evolve to discovery of the grounds, facts, evidence and reasons to demonstrate that a contractual claim does exist.

It is possible that some Contractors do not realise the extent of proof necessary to convince the Architect and his Quantity Surveyor that a contractual claim exists. Before a judge or arbitrator, a civil standard of proof is necessary and it is argued that a lower standard cannot be accepted by an Architect or his Quantity Surveyor.

The standard of civil proof is not as demanding as for a standard of criminal proof. Nevertheless, it is sufficiently demanding in its own right of being equal to the 'balance of probabilities'.

In the very interesting case of *Regina v Swaysland* (1987)(CA), the 'balance of probabilities' was interpreted as meaning that 'it was more likely than not' or 'more probable than not'. The decision in the case of *Dean v Dean* (1986) (CA) is equally important.

However, in the case of *Gibbons and Another v Wall* (1988), the Judge pointed out that the civil standard of proof was flexible and in the case before him, the standard to be applied was at the high end of the range! In *West Oxfordshire District Council v Beratec Ltd* (1986), the Judge stated, concerning the 'balance of probabilities', that the Court 'should not regard that burden having been discharged unless the evidence adduced had been cogent and convincing'. In the case of *Regina v Heshet (1990)* (CA), it was stated that a trial judge 'should address his mind to the all important question of the quality of the evidence'.

Numbering of clauses

IFC84 uses an arithmetical numbering system for the various clauses and also uses decimals to number the sub-clauses and sub-sub-clauses. Fortunately, the decimal system in most instances does not exceed two sets of decimals, viz. sub-sub-clause 2.4.5., but a few exceptions can be found, including alphabetical lettering in Clause 6, ie 6.3A.3.1. or 6.3A3.2. This system is unique to JCT contracts.

Alphabetical footnotes occur throughout the contract and sometimes they are enumerated as well, eg J.1. on Page 17.

Contents of IFC84
1. ARTICLES OF AGREEMENT
2. RECITALS
3. ARTICLES
4. TESTIMONIUM OR ATTESTATION
5. CONDITIONS:
   (a) Intention of parties
   (b) Possession and completion
   (c) Control of the works
   (d) Payment
   (e) Statutory obligations, etc.
   (f) Injury, damage and insurance
   (g) Determination
   (h) Interpretation, etc.
   (i) Settlement of disputes - arbitration
   (j) Appendix
   (k) Supplemental conditions In addition to the standard form of contract itself there are also the following separate documents:

     (i) JCT fluctuations clauses and formula rules;
     (ii) NAM/SC - Sub-contract Conditions for Sub-contractors named under IFC84;
     (iii) Form of Tender and Agreement (NAM/T);
     (iv) Sub-contract formula rules for Named Sub-contractors under IFC84 (NAM/SC/FR);
     (v) ESA/1 - For use between the Employer and a specialist to be named under IFC84.

In addition to these documents, there are also those for domestic Sub-contractors (clauses 3.2, 3.2.1. and 3.2.2.) issued by the Building Employers Confederation.

The settlement of disputes between the Employer and the Contractor is by means of arbitration as set out in Article 5.1. and clause 9.

The documents referred to in the list of contents are usually referred to as the 'Terms and Conditions of the Contract'.

Practice Note IN/1

Attention is specifically drawn to the JCT Practice Note IN/1 which consists of introductory remarks on IFC84. Although not a contract document or a document of contractual reference, it is worthy of careful reading as it provides an understanding of the original thinking which lay behind the creation of the form. The Contractor should also refer to the endorsement sheet on the back of the contract cover which gives guidance on the use of the form. Again, although not an actual contract clause, it is of use in understanding the suitability and purpose of the contract. Similarly, Practice Note 20 *Deciding on the appropriate form of JCT main contract* is equally informative.

Contract documents

Since IFC84 is a hybrid form of contract because it can be used with or without quantities, with a selection of drawings, a specification or schedules of work or bills of quantities prepared by the Architect or Quantity Surveyor, or with a schedule of rates prepared by and submitted by the successful tenderer - the contract document will vary from project to project and be dependent on the specific demands of the project for which it is used. These various contract documents and their alternatives are dealt with under Recitals 1 and 2 and will be considered in detail in the commentary on the Recitals themselves. The contract documents may include some of the following:

(a) contract drawings;
(b) contract specification;
(c) contract schedules of work;
(d) contract bills;
(e) contract sum analysis;
(f) schedules of rates (prepared by the Contractor);
(g) contract agreement;
(h) contract articles of agreement;
(i) contract conditions;
(j) contract appendix;
(k) supplemental conditions.

Clause 1.3. makes it absolutely clear that nothing contained in the contract documents shall over-ride or modify the application of that which is contained in the Articles, Conditions, Supplemental Conditions or Appendix.

The contract documents are cross-referenced to clauses 8.1., 8.2., 8.3., 8.4. and 8.5. for 'Interpretation' or 'Definition'.

Applicability and relevance of IFC84

Practice Note 20 (Revised) considers that IFC84 is most suitable for contracts of not more than twelve months' duration and where the value of the works is not more than £250,000 (at 1984 prices). However, it is permissible to use it for longer and larger contracts, providing the criteria on the endorsement sheet are met. The three criteria for using the form are:

(a) that it is a simple project involving the recognised basic trades and skills of the industry;

(b) that it is without any building service installation of a complex nature or other specialist work of a similar nature;

(c) that it is adequately specified, or specified and billed, as appropriate prior to the invitation of tenders.

Practice Note IN/1 also states that the contract can be used with contract drawings and either a specification or schedules of work, or bills of quantities. Unlike the standard form, it provides for a named person to be employed as a Sub-contractor by the Contractor for work to be priced by the Contractor, but it does not provide for a Sub-contractor to be 'nominated' in respect of a prime cost sum item, nor does it provide for nominated suppliers. IFC84 only provides for fluctuations in respect of contribution, levy and tax, except for those contracts which have a priced bill of quantities, where the 'formula price adjustment' may be used if so desired. The contract may be used as either 'without quantities' or 'with quantities'.

The events which may give rise to a possible extension of time, ie clause 2.3., are somewhat limited in scope when compared with JCT80.

There is no provision for the confirmation of instructions given orally by the Architect. IFC84 does not have a partial possession clause, but Practice Note IH/1, on page 10, gives the draft of a partial possession clause, which may be added to the contract as clause 2.11. if so wished by the Architect.

By contrast there are four new provisions which are of importance:

(i) provision for the Employer to defer giving possession to the site for up to six weeks from the date for possession stated in the Appendix to the Conditions;

(ii) specific provision for the Architect to make under certain circumstances an extension of time after the due completion date has passed;

(iii) provisions relating to the testing of similar work, materials or goods where defects are discovered in work already executed or materials or goods already supplied;

(iv) an optional provision for referring disputes on points of law to the High Court.

The Contractor should make himself fully aware of the contents of Practice Note IN/1 as well as Practice Note 20.

The Agreement

On page 1 of the contract there is the heading 'This Agreement'. Clauses 8.1., 8.2. and 8.3. refer to 'Articles of Agreement' so quite obviously they are expressly given in the contract clauses under the heading of 'Interpretation'.

The blanks on page 1 are for giving the date of when the contract is made and for the names of the two contracting parties. The Employer's name and address are given first and is hereinafter to be called the 'Employer'. The Contractor's name and address is then given and is thereafter called the 'Contractor'. Whenever reference is made to the 'Employer' or 'Contractor', it is known from the Agreement who they are and where they can be located, to allow the issue of notices, instructions, certificates or documents. Where it is stated on page 1 of the contract that 'This Agreement is made the .... day of .... 19..........' the date must be that date when the Employer wrote to the Contractor accepting his tender, ie the precise date (and time) when the Employer posted his letter of acceptance. There is often much confusion over the date when the contract is actually created but this was decisively established in the cases of *Henthorn v Fraser (1892)* and *Adams v Lindsell (1818)*.

The subsequent signing of the contract on page 5 is only confirmation of the fact that the contract has already been made.

The Contractor may withdraw his offer up to, but not after, the acceptance letter from the Employer has been posted, ie once the acceptance letter has been posted the Contractor cannot legally withdraw his offer.

RECITALS AND ARTICLES
Contracts usually have Recitals and Articles and IFC84 is no exception. They serve a very useful purpose by interpreting or construing differences in the construction of obscure clauses. Similarly, side notes or side headings assist in interpreting clauses. In regard to the question of interpretation generally, concerning 'references to clauses', clause 8.1. states that *'unless specifically stated as a reference in the Articles of Agreement, the Conditions, the Supplemental Conditions or the Appendix to any clause, means that clause in the Conditions or the Supplemental Conditions'*.

It is also necessary for the Articles, etc., to be read as a whole, as stated in clause 8.2.. The effect or operation of any article or clause in the Conditions or the Supplemental Conditions or item in the Appendix must, therefore, (unless otherwise specifically stated), be read subject to any relevant qualification or modification in any other Article, or any of the clauses in the Conditions, the Supplemental Conditions or item in or entry in the Appendix.

Recitals
A Recital is an introductory statement explaining the necessity for a contract. It precedes the operative part of a contract and which is given later in the Articles and not overlooking the 'Conditions' annexed hereto.

The two Recitals in IFC84 are preceded by the conjunctions 'whereas' which, according to Chambers' Twentieth Century Dictionary, has the meaning of 'when in fact' or 'taking into consideration' or 'in view of' or 'the fact that'. Therefore, 'whereas' refers to the procedures of tendering and possible negotiation by the Employer with the tenderer between the submission of his tender before it is accepted, that is to say 'in view of all that has taken place, an agreement has now been made between the two contracting parties'.

Recital 1

Recital 1 gives the nature of the works to be executed and the address of the site where they are to be carried out. Recital 1 has a heading of 'the Works'. (Incidentally, the name and address of the Architect and Quantity Surveyor are given in Articles 3 and 4).

Throughout the contract, reference is made to 'the Works' but the only place they are defined is in the first Recital. It is a very important definition since it has major implications for the initiation and origination of contractual claims. Should the Contractor be asked to perform work not included in the contractual definition of 'the Works', star items as well as star rates may be invoked.

Following on from the definition of 'the Works', the Contractor is informed that they *are to be carried out under the direction of the Architect or the Contract Administrator named in Article 3 hereunder and who has caused the certain documents to be prepared showing and describing 'the Works'*.

Clause 8.4. is cross-referenced to Recital 1 in footnote (a). Clause 8.4. states that where the person named in Article 3 is entitled to the name Architect under and in accordance with the Architects (Registration) Acts (1931 to 1969), the term 'the Contract Administrator' shall be deemed to have been deleted throughout the contract. Where the person named is not so entitled, the term the Architect' shall be deemed to have been deleted, ie, mutatis mutandis.

It is proposed to use the term 'the Architect' throughout this publication.

Whilst Recital 1 clearly indicates that there will always be contract drawings there are, however, alternatives to the three other contract documents, ie:
  (i) the specification;
 (ii) the schedule of work;
(iii) bills of quantities.

Footnote (b) provides for the deletion of any of these, always assuming one document must be used.

Recital 1 then subsequently states, after the works 'Bills of Quantities', *'and in respect of any work described and set out therein for pricing by the Contractor and for what the Contractor is required to employ a named person as Sub-contractor in accordance with clause 3.3.1. of the Conditions annexed hereto, has provided all of the particulars of the tender of the named person for that work in a Form of Tender and Agreement NAM/T with Sections I and II completed with the Numbered Documents referred to therein'*. (Note the commentary regarding 'named persons' in clauses 3.3.1. to 3.3.8.)

Footnote (c) allows this part of Recital 1 to be deleted if no items specifying a named person are included in the documents.

On page 2 of Practice Note IN/1, reference is made to deletions and the like by stating *'In the Recitals, the Articles and the Appendix there are spaces for insertions to be made and alternative wording, or paragraphs, for deletion of whichever does not apply, but in the Conditions no insertions are required (unlike the Minor Works Form), nor deletions (unlike the Standard Form).'*

Recital 2
Recital 2 has the heading 'Pricing by the Contractor'. Beside this heading is footnote (d) which requires either alternative 'A' or alternative 'B' to be deleted. Footnote (b) provides for the deletion of either 'A' or 'B'.

Alternative 'A'
Recital 2, alternative 'A' states that the Contractor has priced one of the following contract documents:
  (i) specification;
 (ii) schedules of work;
(iii) bills of quantities.

Bills of quantities, after they have been priced, are contractually referred to as the contract bills.

Recital 2 then goes on to state that *'the total of such a pricing is the 'Contract Sum' as mentioned in Article 2 hereof'.*

The second paragraph of alternative 'A' additionally states *'and such priced document and the Contract Drawings, both signed by or on behalf of the parties (together with, where applicable, the particulars, referred to in the first recital, of the tender of any named person in a certified copy of a Form of Tender and Agreement NAM/T with Sections I and II completed, also signed by or on behalf of the parties hereto), the Agreement and the Conditions annexed thereto are hereinafter called the Contract Documents'.* (See the commentary on clauses 1.2., 1.3., 1.4., 1.5. and 1.6. Note also clause 8.3. (Definitions).)

The hybrid nature of IFC84 can be clearly seen by the alternatives from which the contract documents may be chosen, as well as those in Alternative 'B'.

Practice Note IN/1 (on page 3) indicates that alternatives 'A' and 'B' are 'mutually exclusive alternatives'. It goes on to state that alternative 'A' is for use when the contract documents include a specification or schedule of work or bills of quantities prepared on the instruction of the Employer, which the Contractor has priced in detail and the total of which pricing is the contract sum.

The Practice Note also states on page 3 that *'Schedules of Work are defined in clause 8.3. as a Schedule referring to the Works which has been provided by the Employer; and it is to be distinguished from a Schedule of Rates which the Contractor is to provide where Alternative 'B' applies, unless a Contract Sum Analysis is requested instead'.* (Both are possibly needed.)

Further, the Practice Note states that the form and content of the specification/schedules of work are not prescribed but that they are mentioned in clause 1.2. as defining the quality of the work included in the contract sum where there are no contract bills. When the descriptive document consists of priced bills of quantities IFC84 follows the standard form with quantities in calling these 'the contract bills'. It also requires them to have been prepared in accordance with the Standard Method of Measurement, unless otherwise stated, and providing that the quality and the quantity of work included in the contract sum shall be deemed that which is set out in the contract bills.

Alternative 'B'

Alternative 'B' deals with the contract on the principles of a 'specification and drawings contract'.

Alternative 'B' states that the Contractor has '*stated the sum he will require for carrying out the Works shown on the Contract Drawings and described in the Specification and these documents, both signed by or on behalf of parties (together with, where applicable, the particulars, referred to in the first recital, if the tender of any named person in a certified copy of a Form of Tender and Agreement NAM/T with Sections I and II completed, also signed by or on behalf of the parties hereto), the Agreement and the Conditions annexed hereto are hereafter called the Contract Documents*'. (See also clause 8.3. - Definitions).

Alternative 'B' then goes on to state that the Contractor has supplied the Employer with '*either a Contract Sum Analysis or a Schedule of Rates on which the Contract Sum is based*'.

However, it is possible that the Employer may require both a contract sum analysis and a schedule of rates, since the former without the latter is of little use in the pricing or valuing of variation star items or star rates. Further, contract documents which do not properly provide for variations under clauses 3.7. to 3.7.6. (and in particular clause 3.7.1.) would not really meet the requirements of the contract itself. The contract sum analysis and the schedule of rates would become contractual documents of reference. An example of a contract sum analysis is given in Figure 2.1..

It is clear that there are five choices under either alternative 'A' or 'B', viz.
 (i) specification;
(ii) schedule of rates (schedules provided by the Architect or Quantity Surveyor);
(iii) bills of quantities (provided by the Quantity Surveyor;
(iv) contract sum analysis (provided by the Contractor);
 (v) schedule of rates (provided by the Contractor).

There should be a clear distinction contractually between a schedule of rates prepared by the Architect for the Contractor to price and a schedule of rates prepared and priced by the Contractor - which is quite usual on a specification and drawings contract (Note the commentary to clause 1.2.).

On page 3 of Practice Note IN/1 it states in regard to alternative 'B' that it is for use with drawings and a specification, where the Contractor has not been required to price the specification in detail but has been required to provide a contract sum analysis or a schedule of rates on which the contract sum is based. It also states that '*Under Alternative 'B' the descriptive document consists of the Specification and the Intermediate Form which follows the Standard Form 'Without Quantities' by requiring the Contractor to supply another document, which can be used for valuing variations and provisional sum work*'. This other document may be either a schedule of rates (like the standard form) or a contract sum analysis. Again, it was not considered necessary to give any further

Table 2.1. Example of contract sum analysis

Preliminaries	£	£
Supervision	10,000	
Accommodation:		
(a) Contractor	2,500	
(b) Clerk of works	1,500	
Plant	9,000	
Access to site and temporary roads	2,000	
Local Authority rates	450	
Telephone and calls	750	
Electricity, lighting and power cables	1,000	
Scaffolding	5,000	
Testing, etc.	200	
Watching	750	
Sanitation	1,000	
Welfare	750	
Canteen	800	
Leave perfect on completion	500	
Insurance	2,000	
Water	600	38,800
Works-on-site		3,000
Excavation		18,000
Concrete work		14,500
Brickwork & blockwork		18,000
Roofing		8,000
Carpentry, joinery & ironmongery		39,000
Metalwork		3,200
Floor, wall & ceiling finishings		19,000
Plumbing		7,000
Glazing		2,000
Painting & decorating		5,000
Drainage		9,000
External works & fencing		8,000
Provisional sums		50,500
Provisional quantities		6,000
Builders work in connection with named sub-contractors		4,000
Contract sum		£ 253,000

definition of the specification or schedule of rates. The contract sum analysis is defined in clause 8.3. as *an analysis of the Contract Sum provided by the Contractor in accordance with the stated requirements of the Employer.*

Signing of contract documents

In addition to the signing of the contract documents by the contracting parties themselves, it is quite usual to request the Architect and the Quantity Surveyor to sign the drawings and/or specification and/or bills of quantities and schedules of rates (when prepared by the Architect or Quantity Surveyor). The contract sum analysis or schedule of rates on which the contract sum is based is prepared by the Contractor and should always be signed by him as evidence that the documents were prepared and priced by the Contractor himself.

Since it is always necessary to have a schedule of rates prepared by the Contractor on specification and drawings contracts it might be better to have the conjunction 'or' replaced by conjunction 'and', because under these circumstances, it is imperative to have supplied the Employer with both a contract sum analysis and a schedule of rates. A contract sum analysis presumably does not contain contract rates and prices as would be the case with contract bills of quantities. It would be particularly helpful if the schedule of rates was based on the Standard Method of Measurement, which would implicitly demonstrate the item coverage of the specific rates given. (Note the commentary to clause 3.7.1.)

The Articles

The five Articles which follow after the legal phrase *'Now it is hereby agreed as follows'*, set out the terms and conditions of an English legal contract because the Articles are the operative part of the contract.

A simple legal binding contract consists of three elements. They are offer, acceptance and consideration. When a Contractor submits his tender to an Employer and the Employer writes to the Contractor accepting his tender, the contract is made.

Clause 8.2. states that the Articles of Agreement, the Conditions, the Supplemental Conditions and Appendix are to be read as a whole. The effect on operation of any article or clause in the conditions or the Supplemental Conditions or item in or entry in the Appendix must, therefore, unless otherwise expressly stated, be read subject to any relevant qualification or modification in any other Article or any of the other clauses in the Conditions, the Supplemental Conditions or item in or entry in the Appendix.

Examples of such exceptions are given in Article 5.1. concerning clause A7 of the Supplemental Conditions for Value Added Tax or clause B8 of the Supplemental Conditions for Statutory Tax Deduction Scheme.

The five Articles are concerned with:
(a) Contractor's obligation;
(b) contract sum;
(c) the naming of the Architect;
(d) the naming of the Quantity Surveyor;
(e) arbitration.

Article 1

Article 1 states, '*For the consideration mentioned in Article 2 the Contractor will upon and subject to the Contract Documents carry out and complete the Works*'. The side note to Article 1 reads, '*Contractors obligation*'.

The opening words of Article 1 relate to one of the three elements of a simple or plain legal agreement, ie 'consideration', which is legally defined in *Currie v Misa(1895)* or *Thomas v Thomas (1842)*, as '*some right, interest, profit or benefit occurring to one party or some forbearance, detriment, loss or responsibility given, supplied or undertaken by the other party*'. This definition shows legally that consideration is not solely 'money'.

Consideration can be a very complicated legal problem as is instanced in the case of *Williams v Roffrey Bros & Nicholls (Contractors) Ltd (CA) (1990)*. The preposition 'upon' possibly implies, 'axis, means, pivot, bases, connection with or native to the phrase 'upon and subject to the Contract Documents'.

The Contractor is required by Article 1 to carry out and complete the works. This means that the Contractor, no matter how financially onerous the execution of the works may be, must nevertheless complete them. He cannot commence and carry out some of the works and then, because of exorbitant cost, just walk off the site. If he did so, he would have his employment upon the contract determined under clause 7.1., which is much more likely to be more expensive than completing the works. The works are defined in Recital 1 and in accordance with the contract documents identified in the 2nd Recital, which is in two mutually exclusive alternatives denoted 'A' and 'B'. (See Practice Note IN/1/84, page 3.) The Practice Note goes on to state that '*in either case, the Contract Documents are defined as the Agreement, and the Conditions and the Contract Drawings and one other document describing the items of work*'.

This statement, however, does not completely comply with the demands of clause 8.2., which clause must be followed in reference to the statement in the Practice Note.

The requirements of the second Recital must also be met. (Note the commentary to the Second Recital.) It must also be recognised that the consideration is only payable if the works strictly conform to the contract documents.

Article 2

Article 2 is concerned with the payment of the contract sum. It states that '*the Employer will pay to the Contractor the sum of exclusive of VAT (hereinafter called 'the Contract Sum') or such other sum as shall become payable hereunder at the times and in the manner specified in the Conditions*'. The amount of the contract sum is the quantification of the consideration referred to in Article 1. The reference to a 'contract sum' demonstrates that IFC84 is a lump sum contract, since clauses 3.7 and 4.5. deal with the financial adjustment of the contract sum by addition or deduction as the circumstances dictate and also brought about by the conditions of contract. The nature of a 'lump sum contract' is defined in the legal decision of *London Steam Stone Saw Mills v Lorden (1990)* and is clearly distinguished from a 'measure and value contract as decided in *Jamieson v McInnes* (1887).

The contract sum does not include for VAT (if applicable) and the Contractor is entitled to be paid any VAT in addition to the adjusted contract sum or in everyday language, the final account.

Article 2 goes on to say *'or such other sum as shall become payable hereunder'*. It must be realised that the contract sum can only be adjusted in strict accordance with the conditions of contract.

The more important clauses concerned in the adjustment of the contract sum are given in Table 2.2.

Table 2.2 Clauses concerned with the adjustment of the contract sum

Clause Heading	Clause no.	Add to contract sum	Deduct from Contract sum	Comment
Contract sum	Article 2	Yes	Yes	Definition clause 8.3
Instructions as to inconsistencies errors or omissions	1.4	Yes	Yes	Additions and omissions arising. Correlated to clauses 1.2 and 3.7
Contract bills and SMM	1.5	Yes	Yes	Any departure from SMM correlated to clause 1.4 to be corrected.
Further drawings and details	1.7	Yes	Yes	Variations under clauses 3,6, 3.7 and 3.8
Issue of certificates by the architect	1.9	Yes	Yes	Clauses 2.6, 2.7, 2.8, 2.9, 2.10, 4.5, 4.6, 4.7, 4.8 and 7.1
Unfixed materials or goods	1.10	Yes	Yes	Clause 4.2.1(B)
Off-site materials and goods	1.11	Yes	Yes	Clause 4.2.1(C)
Deferment of possession	2.2	Yes	—	Incurs extension of time
Extensions of time	2.3	Yes	—	Clause 2.4 and 4.12
Certificate of non-completion	2.6	—	Yes	Involves payment of liquidated damages
Liquidated damages for non-completion	2.7	—	Yes	Per week or part thereof actual amount of liquidated damages given in Appendix under clause 2.7
Repayment of liquidated damages	2.8	Yes	—	Clause 2.6 amended
Defects liability	2.10	Yes	—	Possible deduction as well for defects, shrinkage or other faults
Named persons as sub-contractors	3.3.1	Yes	Yes	Clauses 2.3, 3.3.1(a), 3.3.1(b), 3.3.1(c), 3.6, 3.7 and 3.11
Architect's instructions	3.5.1	Yes	Yes	Clause 3.5.2
Variations	3.6	Yes	Yes	Clause 3.6.1, 3.6.2. Definitions of variations
Valuation of variations and provisional sum work	3.7	Yes	Yes	Clauses 3.7.1, 3.7.2, 3.7.3, 3.7.4, 3.7.5, 3.7.6, 3.7.7, 3.7.8, and 3.7.9
Daywork	3.7.5	Yes	—	Main contractor's prime cost as well as for the Electrical Contractors Association and the Heating and Ventilating Contractors Association

Table 2.2 continued

Clause Heading	Clause no.	Add to contract sum	Deduct from Contract sum	Comment
Instructions to expend provisional sum	3.8	Yes	Yes	Clause 3.7
Levels and setting out	3.9	—	—	Errors in setting out
Work not forming part of the contract	3.11	—	—	Clauses 6.1 and 6.3
Instructions as to inspection and tests	3.12	Yes	—	Where the inspection or test shows the materials, goods or work were in accordance with the contract; also any additional inspections and testing. Clause 3.14
Instructions following failure of work etc.	3.13.1	—	—	3.13.2
Refence to arbitration	3.13.2	Yes	—	Award in favour of the contractor. Article 5.1 and clause 9.1
Postponement	3.15	Yes	—	Clauses 2.4.5, 4.11 and 4.12
Adjustment of the contract sum	4.1	Yes	Yes	Clause 1.4. Limitation of adjustments to the contract sum
Interim payments	4.2.2	Yes	Yes	Amounts to be added to or deducted from the contract sum
Practical completion	4.3	Yes	Yes	Amounts to be added or deducted from the contract sum
Retention	4.4	Yes	Yes	Amounts to be added or deducted from the contract sum
Computation of adjusted contract sum	4.5	Yes	Yes	Amounts to be added or deducted from the contract sum
Issue of final certificate	4.6	Yes	Yes	Clause 4.5
Fluctuations	4.9	Yes	Yes	Supplemental conditions C and D
Fluctuations	4.10	Yes	Yes	Named persons
Disturbance of regular progress	4.11	Yes	—	Claims
Statutory obligations	5.1	Yes	—	Fees or charges
Emergency compliance	5.4.3.	Yes	—	Instructions
Value Added Tax	5.5	Yes	—	Supplemental condition A
Injury, damage and insurance	6.2.3	—	Yes	Set-off by the employer due to non-payment of premiums
Insurance liability etc by the employer	6.2.4	Yes	—	Insurance premiums if paid by the contractor
Insurance of the works	6.3.A.2	—	Yes	Set-off by the employer due to non-payment of premiums
Insurance claim	6.3.A.4.4.	Yes	Yes	Payment by the insurers for loss or damage to the works

Table 2.2 continued

Insurance of the works by the employer (new building) claim	6.3.B.3.5.	Yes	–	This claim is treated as a variation by the architect, under clause 3.6
Insurance of the works by the employer (works in, or extensions to, existing structures)	6.3.C.4.4	Yes	–	This claim is treated as a variation by the architect under clause 3.6
Employer's loss of liquidated damages due to extensions of time granted for insurance damage	6.3.D.4	Yes	–	Amount of the premium paid by the contractor

The second Article also refers to such other sum as shall become payable hereunder *'at the times and in the manner specified in the Conditions'*. The question of time correlates to clause 4.2. and also to the Appendix, which is cross-referenced, and states *'Period of interim payments if interval is not one month'*. To all intents and purposes, all interim certificates should cover not less than one calendar month. If a lunar month was intended, this would have been stated in the contract. It is also non-contractual to issue certificates for less than one month. This is occasionally encountered during the currency of a contract and could embarrass some Employers who had agreed a cash flow with their banks based on monthly certificates. An 'early' certificate could be a problem if defective work is not discovered within the period of an 'early' certificate but which would have been detected during a monthly certificate.

In regard to 'early' certificates, it may be said that clause 4.2. and the Appendix are more honoured in their breach than in their observance.

The phrase *'in the manner specified in the Conditions'*, could relate to the holding of retentions, the release of a moiety and then the entire release of retention. It would also provide for payments of claims, whether in part or in whole, as well as VAT and price fluctuations in accordance with the contract.

Article 3
The third Article states that the term 'the Architect' in the Conditions shall mean the person referred to in the first Recital. The name and the address of the Architect is written into the blank space. It has already been pointed out that 'words or terms of art' are used to indicate that they mean the same where used throughout the contract unless, as clause 8.2. informs, *'otherwise specifically stated to be each subject to any relevant qualification or modification'*.

The Architect refererred to in Article 3 means the person whose authority is given in various clauses in the conditions, eg clauses 1.1., 1.4., etc..

After the name and address of the Architect, the third Article goes on to state *'or in the event of his death or ceasing to be so appointed for the purpose of this Contract such other person as the Employer shall within 14 days of the death or cessation nominate for that purpose not being a person to whom the Contractor shall object for reasons thought to be sufficient by an Arbitrator appointed in accordance with Article 5'.*

The Contractor would, of necessity, have very sound reasons for objecting to the appointment of a new Architect. The standard of civil proof being that such reason advised by the Contractor is sufficient to satisfy an arbitrator. Footnote (E) to the third Article, which appears on page 2 of the contract, states *'Strike out the words in italics in Article 3 when the Architect is an official of the Local Authority'*. The words in italics being *'not a person .... in accordance with Article 5'*.

Footnote (A) requires either the 'Architect' or 'Contract Administrator' to be deleted from the third Article. (Note clause 8.4.)

The final sentence to the third Article states, *'Provided no person subsequently so appointed under this Contract shall be entitled to disregard or over-rule any certificate or instruction given by any person for the time previously appointed.'* This is very important and should be always in the mind of the Contractor, since it is quite often the case that a renominated Architect will, for his own reasons, wish to alter or change decisions of the previous Architect. This must be resisted at all costs, as it is a fundamental issue of the third Article. It is suggested that only an arbitrator in an arbitration hearing can change a previous Architect's decisions. (Note the wide scope of the arbitrator's powers in clause 9.3.)

On the other hand, should the Contractor disagree with the Architect over an issued instruction, he may challenge the instruction under clause 3.5.2. and if necessary be referred to immediate arbitration. (Note Article 5.1.)

Failure by the Employer to renominate a fresh Architect promptly is a serious breach of contract and has resulted in at least two legal cases, viz of *Croudace v London Borough of Lambeth* (1984) (CA) and the *London Borough of Merton v Stanley Hugh Leach Ltd (1985)* both of which cases resulted in the favour of the Contractor.

Article 4
The side heading to the fourth Article relates to 'the Quantity Surveyor'. Article 4 itself states that *'the Quantity Surveyor in the Conditions shall mean '...'* and requires the name of the Quantity Surveyor and his address to be given in the blank spaces provided. Article 4 makes it crystal clear that wherever in the Conditions a reference is made to the Quantity Surveyor as a word of art, it is to the person named in the contract under Article 4. (See clauses 3.7., 4.2., 4.5. or 4.11.)

After the name and address of the Quantity Surveyor, Article 4 goes on to state that *'in the event of his death or ceasing to be the Quantity Surveyor for the purpose of this Contract, such other person as the Employer shall nominate for that purpose, not being a person to whom the Contractor shall object for reasons considered to be sufficient by an Arbitrator appointed in accordance with Article 5'.* The possible objection by the Contractor of the fresh Quantity Surveyor by virtue of footnote (E) is to be struck out when the Quantity Surveyor is an official of the local authority.

It will be observed, by contrast, that the new Quantity Surveyor is not restricted in any way concerning the decisions of the first Quantity Surveyor. Nevertheless, the new Quantity Surveyor cannot, nolens volens, arbitrarily alter the previous decisions of the original Quantity Surveyor one way or the other.

Article 5
The fifth Article is concerned with the settlement of disputes by means of arbitration. Article 5.1. is correlated to clause 9. (Note the commentary on this clause.) Immediate arbitration is possible under Article 5.1. since the Article states *'either during the progress or after the completion or abandonment of the Works or the determination of the employment of the Contractor'*.

As has already been mentioned, there are limits to arbitration, because under Supplemental Conditions for VAT (clauses A7.1., A7.2. and A7.3.) an appeal is made to the Commissioners of Customs and Excise.

Under clause A10, the arbitration provision is restricted to any matters to be dealt with under clause A4.

The exception to arbitration lies in the specific requirements of the statutory tax deduction scheme given in the Act of Parliament or any other Act of Parliament or statutory instrument, rule or order made under an Act of Parliament which may provide for some other method of resolving such dispute or difference. This could mean appearing before the Commissioners of Inland Revenue.

The Appendix has the choice of having clause 9.6. applying or not. Clause 9.6. contemplates the problem of whether the same arbitrator who dealt with an arbitration between the Employer and the Main Contractor should also be the same arbitrator to hear an arbitration between the Main Contractor and a Sub-contractor on a related dispute. Presumably this could be a pre-contract agreement between the Main Contractor and the Employer.

In the case of *Northern Regional Health Authority v Derek Crouch Construction Co Ltd and Crown House Engineering Ltd (Nominated Sub-Contractors* (1984) (CA) (which was concerned with a JCT63 form of contract), it was established that an arbitrator could be the same arbitrator in two separate cases of arbitration between the Main Contractor (Derek Crouch Construction Co Ltd) and the Employer, as well as the different arbitration between the nominated Sub-contractor (Crown House Engineering Ltd) and the Employer (because of the arbitration clause 8(b) in the green form). A similar process is available under clause 9.6. of IFC84.

It is imperative for the Contractor to decide whether he really wishes to go to arbitration (under Article 5.1.) or litigation (note clause 4.11.) because in the case of *Turner & Goundy (A Firm) v McConnell and Another* (1985) the Contractor first of all decided to go to litigation then changed his mind and tried to revert to arbitration. However, the Judge refused to allow the Contractor to go to arbitration because he had taken the first step in litigation and was now debarred from going to arbitration.

(Note clause 9.5. which allows both contracting parties to either appeal or to apply to the High Court on questions of law.)

The decision in the case of *Hayter v Nelson and Others* (1990) held that in the context of an arbitration, the words 'disputes' and 'differences' were applicable to cases, even where it could be there and then determined that one party or another was in the right.

TESTIMONIUM OR ATTESTATION

The attestation clause to IFC84 is given on page 5 and provides for the statement that the contract has been duly executed in the presence of witnesses. The purpose of attestation is to testify to its genuineness. The attestation clause is preceded by the legal phrase *'as witness the hands of the parties hereto'*, which is self-explanatory. The signatures may be the actual contracting parties themselves or their nominees.

There are three footnotes to the attestation clause.

Footnote (   ) states that it is for an Agreement executed under hand (ie a simple or plain contract).

Footnote (*) states that it is for an Agreement executed under seal by an individual or incorporated body.

Footnote (**) states that it is for an Agreement executed under seal by a local authority, a company or other body corporate.

THE APPENDIX

With IFC84, it is appropriate to consider the Appendix now and not later on, as would normally be the procedure. This is because the choice of alternatives is given in the Appendix and not in the text of the contract.

Footnote (n) states 'Delete as applicable' and correlates to clauses 2.4.10.,2.4.11., 2.2., 2.4.14., 4.11.(a), 4.9.(b) Part I/Part II of Section 2 of the formula rules to apply under D1, 6.2.4., 6.3.1., 6.3D, 9.1. and 9.6.

The choice of which alternative is selected would be a matter decided between the Employer and the Architect, because it is best suited to the needs of the contract.

The nature of the possible options are as follows:

Clause 2.4.10.
whether to grant an extension of time or not for a possible delay caused by the Contractor's inability to obtain essential labour which could not have been foreseen at the time of tender;

Clause 2.4.1.
whether to grant an extension of time or not for a possible delay caused by the Contractor's inability

to obtain essential goods or materials which could not have been foreseen at the time of tender;

Clauses 2.2., 2.4.14. and 4.11.(a).
whether or not to allow the Employer to delay giving full possession of the site for a period up to six weeks, calculated from the date of possession given in the Appendix;

Clause 4.9.(b).
formula fluctuations can only apply if there are bills of quantities of the contract. There is, however, a choice to have either the formula fluctuations (Supplemental Condition D) or the Contribution, levy and tax fluctuations (Supplemental Condition C). If the formula fluctuations are chosen, then a decision also has to be made whether or not to use Part I or Part II of Section 2 of the formula rules.

Part I of Section 2 uses a work category method where there is a separate application of the work category index numbers. Part II of Section 2 uses the weighted work group indices. The non-adjustable element does not apply to the private edition;

Clause 6.2.4.
insurance against injury to persons or property requires a decision as to whether or not the Employer wishes to have a joint names policy for this purpose;

Clause 6.3.1.
there are three choices of which one must be selected, ie, clauses 6.3A., 6.3B. or 6.3C. Footnote (k) to clause 6.3.1. states clause 6.3A. is applicable to the erection of a new building where the Contractor is required to take out joint names policy for all risks insurance.
Clause 6.3B. is applicable where the Employer has elected to take out such joint names policy.
Clause 6.3C. is to be used for alterations of, or extensions to, existing structures under which the Employer is required to take out a joint names policy for all risks insurance for the works and also a joint names policy to insure the existing structures and their contents owned by him or for which he is responsible against loss or damage thereto by the specified perils;

Clause 6.3d.
a decision is needed as to whether insurance may be required or not for circumstances when an extension of time has been granted by the Architect under clause 2.3. by reason of the event under clause 2.4.3. which contemplates loss or damage caused by one or more of the specified perils. A definition of specified perils is given in clause 8.3.; Clause 9.1.

The list of professional institutes given may be reduced if so wished by deleting one or two of the three institutes listed;

Clause 9.6.
the reference to an arbitrator under NAM/SC allows for an arbitration under the main contact and also allows for the same arbitrator to act in an arbitration between the Main Contractor and a

Sub-contractor if of a similar character. It has to be decided under claues 9.6. if this alternative is to be applied or not. (Note the commentary to Article 5.)

Generally

The Appendix may provide the source of some financial success for a contractor as illustrated in the case *Temloc Ltd v Errill Properties Ltd* (1987). This case under the JCT80 had NIL written against the liquidated and ascertained damages clause of the Appendix. The Employer sued for unliquidated damages and lost his appeal court case because Lord Justice Nourse stated '*Clause 24 dealt comprehensively with the Employers' right to damages for late completion whether liquidated or not. It was impossible to attribute to the parties an intention that the Employer should have the option of claiming unliquidated damages when they had expressly agreed that liquidated damages of the same character should be nil*'. The legal term 'liquidated damages' is used in IFC84.

3. CONDITIONS OF CONTRACT

INTRODUCTION

The conditions of contract are prefixed by the legal phrase *'conditions hereinbefore referred to'*, which is a cross-reference to the second Recital, where it states in alternatives 'A' and 'B' that *'the Conditions annexed hereto'* are contractual documents. Article 1 also refers to 'contractual documents which give the Conditions of Contract their legal status, ie, *'hereinbefore referred to'*.

A thorough understanding of the conditions of contract is fundamental in searching out, originating and successfully resolving merited contractual claims.

There are nine basic conditions of contract:
1. Intentions of the parties.
2. Possession and completion.
3. Control of the works.
4. Payment.
5. Statutory obligations, etc.
6. Injury, damage and insurance.
7. Determination.
8. Interpretation.
9. Settlement of disputes - arbitration.

In addition there are four Supplemental Conditions:
A. VAT (clause 5.5.);
B. Statutory tax deduction scheme (clause 5.6.);
C. Contributions, levy and tax fluctuations (clause 4.9.(a));
D. Use of price adjustment formulae (clause 4.9.(B)).

Supplementary Conditions C and D are in separate booklets to the main contract conditions.

Clause B7 should be noted in particular since it states that *'if compliance with this Supplemental Condition involves the Employer or the Contractor in not complying with any other provisions of the Contract, then the provisions of this Supplemental Contribution shall prevail'*.

The nine conditions are sub-divided into numerous clauses, some of which only amount to five clauses, whilst others run to fifteen.

If a contract has particularly difficult or onerous conditions, the contracting party who in seeking to enforce those conditions rigorously is required by common law to be capable of showing that they have been clearly and fairly brought specifically to the attention of the other contracting party. Failure to do so may result in those difficult or onerous conditions not being considered part of the contract. This doctrine of common law was decided in the case of *Thorton v Shoe Lane Parking (1971)(CA)* and also in *Interfoto Picture Library Ltd v Stilleto Visual Programmes Ltd* (1987).

The Contractor should, therefore, ensure that this is not the circumstance on a contract in hand or when it arises during the currency of an existing contract. Expert legal advice should always be sought from consultants on these issues.

The ensuing commentary on the conditions of contract seeks to bring to the mind of Contractors those clauses which contractually concern successful financial claims. The avoidance of liquidated damages by being granted an extension of time without financial liability for the Employer, whilst a negative claim, is, notwithstanding, of certain financial benefit to a Contractor. It is interesting to observe that out of the nine conditions, the majority provide, one way or the other, for financial benefit to the Contractor. But it is for the Contractor to remain on the alert throughout the contract to seek or claim his contractual rights.

CONDITION 1. INTENTION OF THE PARTIES
The heading to Condition 1 devolves into eleven clauses. The reason for referring to the sub-division of Condition 1 as clauses is founded on internal evidence of the contract. For instance, clause 1.4. itself refers to clause 1.7. and, similarly, clause 1.8. refers to clauses 1.3. and 1.7..

It is always best to attempt to derive explanations from the text of the contract proper, rather than seek external evidence, although from time to time it may be necessary to do so.

Clause 1.1. Contractor's Obligations
Clause 1.1. states *'The Contractor shall carry out and complete the works ...'*. This means that even if the Contractor is running into various difficulties and serious financial losses (for which there is no remedy under the contract), he cannot just 'fold up his tent and disappear into the night', leaving the contract uncompleted. The phrase *'carry out and complete'* legally means that he is bound to complete the contract. If he remains solvent and leaves the site before proper completion he faces those measures which will be enacted against him under clause 7.1.(a) of the determination of the Contractor's employment and its serious fiscal implications.

Clause 1.1. also states that the Contractor is to carry out and complete the works in accordance with the contract documents identified in the second Recital. (Note the commentary already given to the second Recital and whether the 'A' or 'B' alternative was selected.)

It is evident from the first sentence to clause 1.1. that the Contractor is not responsible for the design of the permanent works. This is the function of the Architect and any other consultants. The Contractor is responsible for the design of all temporary works which may consist of earthwork supports, trench sheet piling, heavy sheet piling, shoring, strutting, centring, horsing and strutting, needling, shoring and strutting, formwork, shuttering, scaffolding, hoists, gantries, site roads, walkways, site huts and storage sheds, hoardings, fans, fencing, hardstandings, services, disposal of water, methods of drying out the works, protection of all the permanent and temporary works and attendance on specialists.

Not only is the Contractor liable for the design of temporary works, he is also responsible for seeing that the temporary works are correctly executed. He cannot claim for any collapse of temporary works if not properly executed from his insurers, since insurance policies exclude 'making good faulty or defective materials or workmanship'. (Note the decision in *Kim Barket Ltd v Aegon Insurance Co Ltd and Another* (1990).)

Clause 1.1. after the colon states '*provided that where and to the extent that approval of the quality of materials or of the standards of workmanship is a matter for the opinion of the Architect such quality and standards shall be to the reasonable satisfaction of the Architect*'. This statement can only relate to those materials or workmanship not actually specified in the contract documents.

The Architect cannot contractually accept materials of a lower quality or labour of an inferior standard to that specified in the contract documents. An exception to this fundamental principle is given in clause 2.10. but requires an appropriate deduction from the contract sum as ascertained by the Architect and/or Quantity Surveyor.

Clause 1.2. - Quality and quantity of work
Clause 1.2. delineates the quality and quantity of the work under three different conceptions of contract documents. The possible alternatives also fall into the two broad categories of contracts with or without quantities.

The first concept is given in paragraph one of clause 1.2. and reads, '*Where or to the extent that quantities are not contained in the Specification/Schedules of Work and there are no Contract Bills* (ie a Contract with quantities), *the quality and quantity of the work included in the Contract Sum (stated in Article 2) shall be deemed to be that in the Contract Documents taken together*'. The paragraph then goes on to state, '*provided that if work stated as shown on the Contract Drawings is inconsistent with the description, if any, of that work in the Specification/Schedules of Work then that which is stated or shown on the Contract Drawings shall prevail for the purpose of this clause*'. The latter portion of clause 1.2., paragraph one, gives superiority to the contract drawings over the other contract document, whether it be the specification or the schedule of work. In other words, if the drawings show softwood joinery and the specification or schedule of work call for hardwood joinery, then softwood joinery would prevail by virtue of the contract drawings.

Paragraph one of clause 1.2. must also be read in conjunction with clause 1.4. as far as inconsistencies are concerned.

There may be contractual difficulties over paragraph one as far as a specification and drawings contract is concerned, which are not immediately obvious. The Contractor has to take special care when preparing his estimate in regard to any indispensable or contingent necessary works, whether expressly or implicitly included in the specification or on the contract drawings, especially as the contract drawings prevail. (Note the decision in the case of *Williams v Fitzmaurice* (1858)).

The second concept is given in paragraph two of clause 1.2. and reads, '*Where or to the extent that quantities are contained in the Specification/Schedules of Work and there are no Contract Bills, the quality and quantity of the work included in the Contract Sum for the relevant items shall be deemed to be that which is set out in the specification/schedules of work*. This is a contract with quantities.

It will be observed that there is no mention of the contract drawings in this paragraph but quite clearly from Recitals 1 and 2, alternatives 'A' or 'B', there will be contract drawings in all instances. Paragraph 2 means that either the specification or schedules of work would prevail over the contract drawings.

The third concept is given in paragraph three of clause 1.2. and reads, '*Where there are Contract Bills, the quality and quantity of the work included in the Contract Sum, shall be deemed to be that which is set out in the Contract Bills,*'. This concept is that of a lump sum contract with quantities.

The contractual issue of inconsistencies, errors or omissions in the contract bills is dealt with under clauses 1.4. and 1.5.. The fact that the preambles to the work sections of the contract bills are also 'specification' clauses should not be overlooked.

Clause 1.3. - Priority of contract documents
Clause 1.3. states, '*Nothing contained in the Specification/Schedules of Work/Contract Bills shall over-ride or modify the application or interpretation which is contained in the Articles, Conditions, Supplemental Conditions or Appendix*'.

This is a most important clause, since it establishes the superiority of the contract itself over other contract documents. Unfortunately, the question of the contract drawings is not dealt with in clause 1.3. and leaves the issue open to conjecture.

It will be recalled that in paragraph one of clause 1.2. the contract drawings prevailed over the specification or schedules of work as far as inconsistencies were concerned. It would seem to be the case that, despite the omission of a mention of contract drawings from clause 1.3., they cannot over-ride the contract. The heading to clause 1.3. incidentally is '*Priority of Contract Documents*' and since contract drawings are one of the 'contract documents', this would seem to strengthen the argument.

The priority of the contract over other contract documents has been the subject of several legal cases where the various Courts have upheld its priority, viz *Gleeson (Contractors) Ltd v London Borough of Hillingdon (1970); English Industrial Estates Corporation v George Wimpey and Co Ltd (1972)(CA); Gold v Patman and Fotheringham Ltd (1958); Bramwell & Ogden Ltd v Sheffield City Council (1983); Bickerton and Son Ltd v North West Metropolitan Regional Hospital Board (1969)(CA).*

Examples of where the Architect or Quantity Surveyor might fall into error over this issue would be if the contract bills stated that the rates and prices are deemed to include for all testing of work, goods or materials. This would be in contradiction to clause 3.12., which refers to those of testing items provided for in the contract sum. Hence, the testing of piling would also require a separate item to be measured and included in the contract bills in conformity with either SMM6 clause E8 or SMM7 clause D11. Any test ordered by the Architect which caused work, goods or materials to fail would require the Contractor to re-execute the work at his own cost. (Note the commentary to clauses 3.13.1 and 3.13.2.)

Clause 1.4 - Instructions as to inconsistencies, errors or omissions

Clause 1.4 provides for the Architect to issue instructions in regard to the correction of four possibilities under the conditions of contract.

The heading to clause 1.4, which refers to errors, must obviously relate to errors in the contract drawings, even though only inconsistencies are specifically referred to in the first possibility. The second possibility does specifically refer to any error in the contract documents, which must include the contract drawings. This is unique in the JCT standard form, where usually only errors by Quantity Surveyors are dealt with! It could not be tolerated under the contract for errors in the contract drawings to remain uncorrected!

The first possibility concerns the correction of any inconsistency in or between the contract documents or drawings and documents issued under clause 1.7 and further drawings at clause 3.9 levels. It will be remembered that with any inconsistency in regard to the first concept of clause 1.2, it is the contract drawings which prevail over the other documents. Hence, any other inconsistency not involving the contract drawings would, therefore, be corrected under clause 1.4. All instructions issued by the Architect must be in writing in accordance with clause 3.5.1. The general grounds of inconsistencies in the contract documents could be between:

(a) items on an individual drawing;
(b) the various drawings themselves;
(c) the drawings and other documents;
(d) items in the specifications themselves;
(e) the specification and other documents;
(f) items in the schedule of works;
(g) the schedule of work and other documents;
(h) the various sections of the contract bills themselves;
(i) the contract bills and other documents;
(j) any further drawings and documents issued under clauses 1.7 and 3.9 and the matters of (a) to (i) above. (Whilst not actually referred to, any Architect's instruction which is inconsistent with any of the contract documents must also be corrected by virtue of clause 1.4.).

To be inconsistent must mean that two or more items are 'intrinsically incompatible'. The Architect's instruction must, therefore, correct the inconsistency. Examples could be if the brickwork shown on the drawings as best quality stocks is measured in the contract bills as fletton brickwork, or reinforced concrete beds being shown on the drawings and only plain concrete beds being given in the schedules of work, or copper tubing being shown on the drawings and plastic tubing being measured in the specification (with quantities). The Architect, who has to give a business efficiency to the contract, could cause a delay if he failed to deal simply with the inconsistencies, whether it is his or other persons' faults.

It is in the Contractor's own financial interest to search out all inconsistencies in the contract documents as early on in the contract as he possibly can! The Contractor is not in any breach of contract is he fails to discover any inconsistency, since it is equally incumbent on the Architect to also search out inconsistencies.

Cross-reference should be made to clauses 5.1, 5.2, 5.3 and 5.4 concerning divergencies (inconsistencies) from statutory requirements, where the same legal situation exists. Inconsistencies should not vitiate the contract.

The second possibility requiring correction under clause 1.4 relates to *'any error in description or in quantity or any omission of items in the Contract Documents or in any one of such documents'*. These matters appear to be quite straightforward.

The phrase *'any error in description'* would need the Contractor, in the first instance, to inform the Architect of the nature of the 'error' and to ask for a correction. The 'error' does not obviously relate to an 'error in quantity' as this is a separate issue; neither does it relate to an omission of item(s). There could be an initial error in the General Description of the Works as SMM6 - B.1.2. or SMM7 - A13.

The type of error envisaged could be 'high tensile steel rod reinforcement' instead of 'mild steel rod reinforcement' or 'obscure glass' instead of 'plain glass'.

Errors in quantity would relate to the quantities given in either the specification or schedule of work or the contract bills. The errors in quantity would be that the quantities given in the 'contract documents' are either too low or too high. Doubtless, the Architect would refer these errors to the Quantity Surveyor for his opinion and decision.

If a quantity is too high in the contract bills, its reduction may invoke the question of shortfall, which in turn may affect the contract rate or price by requiring it to be converted to a star rate, which in turn may increase the value of the item. (Note the commentary on clause 3.7.3 which deals with *'any significant change in the quantity of the work set out'*.)

The omission of items in the contract documents will need proof that they have not been included and reasons given for having them now included in the final account, as prepared under clause 4.6.

These omissions may be proven by means of the Standard Method of Measurement. For instance, if a concrete wall above ground level has been measured but no formwork measured to its vertical faces and end, then under SMM6 clause F13.1(a) or SMM7 clause E20.12.1, it can be established the item has been omitted in error from the contract bills.

Other omissions may be discovered by studying the contract drawings and finding that an item or items are not included in the specification or schedule of works measured items, or indeed in the contract bills. It is in the interests of the Contractor to ensure that a rigorous search of the contract documents is made to discover any possible omissions.

(Note the commentary to clause 1.5 which examines the correlation of the contractual documents of reference in regard to the Standard Method of Measurement.)

The third possibility requiring correction under clause 1.4 is concerned with '*any error or omission in the particulars provided by the Employer of the tender of a person named in accordance with clause 3.3.1*'. (Named Sub-contractors.)

There is a 'Tender and Agreement NAM/T' form available for the Main Contractor and the Named Sub-contractor. There is also a RIBA/CASEC - Form of Employer/Specialist Agreement - ESA/1 for use between the Employer and a specialist to be named under IFC84.

The fourth possibility calling for a correction under clause 1.4 deals with '*any departure from the method of preparation of the Contract Bills referred to in clause 1.5*'. Before dealing with the matter in detail, it should perhaps be pointed out that the quantities given in a specification, schedule of work or even the schedule of rates provided by the Contractor under the second Recital - alternative 'B', might well also benefit by being measured in accordance with the Standard Method of Measurement. Otherwise the rates of measurement should be clearly stated in those documents as to that which is to be considered included in the item coverage of the various quantities. Not to do so would leave the question of what is deemed included or not at large.

Clause 1.4 is absolutely clear that in the event of a departure from the Standard Method of Measurement, the Architect must issue instructions requiring the correction of that departure. Not all JCT standard forms are as specific as IFC84 regarding the need to correct such departures from the SMM. This is a sensible step forward in giving a contractual clause for a claim under clause 1.4, and the fourth possibility therein.

What is intended or involved by the phase '*of any departure from the method of preparation of the contract bills*'? It must mean first of all that the Contractor has been placed at a financial disadvantage by reason of the Quantity Surveyor departing from the SMM. Examples of this could be just measuring ordinary excavation in the contract bills instead of measuring excavation in short lengths in underpinning, ie, as SMM6 - clause H1 or SMM7 clause D50, or if the contract bills stated that heavy sheet steel driven interlocking piling was deemed to be included in all earthwork support items under SMM6 - D14 or SMM7 - clause D20.7, instead of correctly measuring under SMM6 - E4.G or SMM7 - D32-2, or the failure to keep work to existing buildings separate from new work, ie, as clause A.9.1 of SMM6 or clauses 7.1(a) and 13 of SMM7 - General Rules, or measuring, cubically, items which should be superficial or measuring superficially items which should be lineal or measuring lineally items which should be enumerated or seeking to include specific items required by the Standard Method be given as separate items into the cubic, superficial or lineal items, ie, 'preparing plans or diagrams of installations as fitted' unless amended in accordance with clause 1.5. In all these departures from the Standard Method, the Contractor must be able to prove that he has suffered financially.

Frequently, the Contractor may not have been put to a financial loss. Supposing the Quantity Surveyor has measured out in detail the items for a staircase which the Standard Method requires to be an enumerated item but nevertheless includes all the items under a heading of 'The following in No. 1 Staircase:'. He has, to all intents and purposes, enumerated the item but in addition has given all the individual items in detail, which does not incur the Contractor in any loss. Additionally, it does provide a means of valuing any variations to the staircase brought about by an Architect's instruction. The fact that a Contractor has, at the time of tender, priced all the individual items in detail and does not raise queries about the manner of measurement, implies that he is perfectly satisfied with the contact bills in this respect. To go even further, as a pure hypothesis, it could be considered in a contract with quantities stated that SMM7 had been used in its preparation, and then only one enumerated item occurred in the contract bills which stated 'No. 1 Cathedral including a Norfolk latch' and the Contractor then priced that single item without any contractual reservation of any kind whatsoever, could the Contractor then complain if his tender was then accepted?

The Contractor should ensure that the General Rules of the SMM are observed. For instance, SMM rule A1 requires in certain instances that more detailed information may be required in order to define the precise nature and extent of the required work. Rule A.5.1(b) requires that all component details are shown on drawings, with all the information necessary for the manufacture and assembly of the component. Rule A.5.1(c) permits a 'bill diagram' to be included in the contract bills to aid the description of the item by way of dimensions or detail. Rule A5.2 provides that *'the requirements of this document for detailed descriptions shall be deemed to have been complied with if drawn information is provided and such information indicates fully the items to be described'*. Similar rules occur in SMM7, ie, rules 1.1, 4.2, 4.7, 5.2, 5.3, 5.4 and 9.1.

The final sentence to the first paragraph of clause 1.4 states *'and no such inconsistency, error or departure shall vitiate this contract'*.

The final paragraph to clause 1.4 states, *'if any such instruction changes the quality or quantity of work deemed to be included in the Contract Sum as referred to in clause 1.2 - (Quality and quantity of work) or changes any obligations or restrictions imposed by the Employer, the correction shall be valued under clause 3.7 (Valuation of Variations).'*

Whilst the last paragraph to clause 1.4 is clear, nevertheless, it questions what changes in obligations or restrictions may arise by correcting inconsistencies, errors or omissions. For instance, if a restriction arose from a correction, assuming that there were no other obligations imposed by the Employer, then an obligation could not be then imposed contractually by the correction instructions.

Of course, the Employer, through his agent the Architect, can vary any obligations or restrictions already contained in the contract bills (observe clause 3.6.2.), but there is no contractual power to create fresh and original obligations or restrictions and variations for items, as this runs counter to the contract itself. (Note the commentary to clause 3.6.2.)

It must be stressed that although clause 1.4 is very broad in regard to the correction of inconsistencies, errors or omissions, clause 4.1 by contrast forbids any correction of the contract sum for any error or omission, whether arithmetic or not, in the computation of the contact sum because it has been deemed to have been accepted by the parties hereto.

If SMM7 is to be used then clause 1.4 should be amended to conform with Amendment 4 to the standard form regarding clause 1.4.

Clause 1.5 - Contract bills and SMM
Clause 1.5 states, '*Where the Contract Documents include Contract Bills, the Contract Bills unless otherwise expressly stated therein in respect of any specified item or items are to have been prepared in accordance with the Standard Method of Measurement of Building Works 6th Edition published by the Royal Institution of Chartered Surveyors and the Building Employers Confederation*'. There is now SMM7 which may be used instead of SMM6, but some Quantity Surveyors still use SMM5 because of difficulty over the drawing clauses of SMM6. Therefore, it is necessary for the Contractor to be aware of which edition is applicable.

The Contractor may be able to found a claim against the Employer if the contract bills do not strictly follow the SMM in every respect. It will be necessary to demonstrate how the failure to follow the SMM has caused the Contractor direct loss and/or expense. If the Quantity Surveyor wishes, for reasons of his own, to depart from the SMM for any specified items, he must clearly draw the attention of the Contractor to the departure. It is usual before measuring the item in the contract bills to state as a preamble that '*the SMM has not been followed in the following item*'. It may be necessary then to give an item coverage to allow the Contractor to understand what is required to be priced for this item.

The publication '*Comments and clarifications on SMM*' which was written with respect to SMM5 applies equally to SMM6 and SMM7. On page 4 of that publication, paragraph 7 (vi), reference is made to the phrase '*unless expressly stated in regard to any specified item or items*'. These words were added with the object of guarding explicitly against a general statement that some items may not be prepared in accordance with the principles of the SMM.

Clause 1.7 - Further drawings and details
Clause 1.7 indicates that not all the contract drawings and details will be available at the time of tender or commencement of the contract. Provision is made contractually for the Architect to provide the Contractor with two copies of such further drawings or details as are reasonably necessary to enable the Contractor to carry out and complete the works in accordance with the conditions. Under the scope of clause 2.4.7, the Contractor can ask for necessary instructions, drawings or details from the Architect which he finds are imperative to allow him to complete the works.

It is a contractual obligation for the Architect to provide all additional necessary drawings and details, especially so because of the legal doctrine of giving a 'business efficacy' to the contract as decided in the cases of *Reigate v Union Manufacturing Co* (1918) or *The Moor Cock* (1889).

Failure by the Architect to provide drawings and details for such issues as are unknown to the

Contractor are of a far graver importance because of the unknown elements it may involve.

If SMM7 is to be used then clause 1.5 should be amended to conform with Amendment 4 to the standard form regarding clause 1.5.

Clause 1.8 -Limits to use of documents

Clause 1.8 sets out the principle of confidentiality of the contract documents by the contracting parties as well as the Architect or Quantity Surveyor.

Table 3.1 Certificates that might be issued under IFC84

Clause	Description
1.9	Issue of certificates
2.3	Extension of time
2.5	Further extensions of time
2.6	Non-completion
2.7	Liquidated damages
2.8	Re-payment of liquidated damages
2.9	Practical completion
2.10	Defects liability discharged
3.2.2.(b)	Interim
3.2.2(c)	Interim
3.2.2(d)	Interim
4.2	Interim
4.2.1.	Interim
4.2.2	Interim
4.3	Interim certificate of practical completion
4.6, 4.7	Final
4.8	Effect of interim (other than final) certificates
5.5	Value Added Tax
5.6	Statutory Tax Deduction Scheme
6.3A.4	Use of insurance monies
7.4(d)	Consequences of determination
7.5.1, 7.5.2	Failure to honour certificates
7.7(b)	Consequences of determination
A2, A4.1	Value Added Tax
B 1.1, B 2.1, B 3.1, B 3.2, B 3.3, B 5.1	Statutory Tax Deducation Scheme

Clause 1.9 - Issue of certificates by Architect

Clause 1.9 states *'except where provided otherwise any payment or other certificate to be issued by the Architect shall be issued to the Employer and a duplicate shall at the same time be sent to the Contractor'.* Certificates should always be in writing and it is surprising that such a stricture is not made in the text of clause 1.9. The Contractor should always insist on a written certificate from the Architect. (Note the commentary to clause 3.5.1.)

The reference in clause 1.9 to *'or other certificate'* indicates that there are a variety of certificates under IFC84.

Clause 1.10 - Unfixed materials or goods; passing of property, etc.

Clause 1.10 deals with two aspects of unfixed materials or goods delivered to site. Firstly, the control of the materials and secondly, with a payment on account certificate and ownership when delivered and placed on site. (Off-site materials and goods are dealt with under clause 1.11.)

The control of unfixed materials or goods is covered in the first paragraph to clause 1.10. Whilst the Contractor may deliver unfixed materials or goods to site and which are placed on or adjacent to the works, they cannot be removed from the site without the Architect giving his written consent to do so. Such consent shall not be unreasonably withheld. The Contractor does not need written consent first to move the materials or goods around the site until finally and permanently placed in position.

Clause 6.3.2 makes it contractually plain that 'site materials' means all unfixed materials and goods delivered to, placed on or adjacent to the works and intended for incorporation therein.

Under clause 4.2.1(b) an interim payment is strictly limited to materials and goods which have been reasonably and properly and not prematurely delivered to or adjacent to the works and which are adequately protected against weather and other exigencies. Failure to protect the materials and goods adequately would be a bar to their inclusion in an interim certificate. (Note the commentary to clause 4.2.1(b).)

The second paragraph to clause 1.10 deals with the ownership of materials or goods when they have been paid for in a payment certificate made by the Employer. Clause 1.10 clearly states that such materials or goods shall become the property of the Employer. Once the materials and goods become the Employer's property, the Contractor shall remain responsible for loss or damage of the same but nevertheless subject to clause 6.3B and 6.3C.2 to .4 (insurance by the Employer). The need of clarity for this issue of the passing of the property from one person to another arose out of the legal dilemma of *Aluminium Industrie Vassen v Romalpa* (1976) where the problem of insolvency was also involved.

However, a domestic Sub-contractor who had not been paid by the Main Contractor for the delivery of Welsh roofing slates to the site was not bound by clause 14(2) in JCT63 (which was similar to clause 1.10 of IFC84) because although the Main Contractor had been paid, the domestic Sub-contractor had not been paid by the Main Contractor. In this case,the contract clause concerning passing the title of property was circumvented. This was the decision in the case of *Dawber Williamson Roofing Ltd v Humberside CC* (1979).

Clause 1.11 - Off-site materials and goods, passing of property, etc.

Clause 1.11 deals with two aspects of unfixed materials or goods not delivered to site. Firstly, the control of the materials and secondly with ownership when included in a payment on account certificate.

The control of unfixed materials or goods stored off-site is covered by the first sentence to clause 1.11, under the provisions of clause 4.2.1(c), which only provides for the inclusion of the value of such materials or goods as are at the discretion of the Architect.

The value of off-site goods and materials at the discretion of the Architect may be considerably less than those on site goods and materials reasonably and properly and not prematurely delivered to or adjacent to the works for incorporation therein. The Contractor may wish to make provision for this financial fact in his tender.

The remainder of clause 1.11 deals with the ownership of materials or goods when they have been paid for in a payment certificate made by the Employer. Clause 1.11 clearly states that such materials and goods become the Employer's property when a payment certificate has been discharged by the Employer and that the Contractor shall not except for the purpose of use on the works remove or cause or permit the same to be moved or removed from the premises where they are kept pro tem. The Contractor is also responsible for any loss thereof or damage thereto and for the cost of storage, handling and insurance of the same until such time as they are delivered to and placed on or adjacent to the works. When off-site materials or goods are delivered to site they then fall under the provisions of clause 1.10.

The legal cases discussed under clause 1.10 similarly apply to clause 1.11. The onus of responsibility lies with the Contractor to ensure that all off-site materials and goods are properly labelled as being the property of the Employer and that the materials and goods are kept securely locked up and bonded on the premises where they are to be safeguarded. Thus, in the question of insolvency of the Contractor or his supplier, the liquidator will not have the power of 'seizure' over these items.

CONDITION 2 - POSSESSION AND COMPLETION
Clause 2.1 Possession and completion dates

The possession of the site shall be given to the Contractor on the date of possession stated in the Appendix. Should there be no date given in the Appendix, then a date will have to be negotiated between the Employer and the Contractor. The second sentence to clause 2.1 sets out the common law situation concerning building contracts, ie, to begin and regularly and diligently proceed with the works and shall complete the same on or before the date stated in the Appendix, subject nevertheless to the provisions for extension of time in clause 2.3.

By knowing the contractual date of possession and the date for completion, the length of the contract period can be legally determined.

The importance of the completion date must not be overlooked. It is preceded by the date of practical completion which is synonymous with the Contractor handing back the site and the works to the Employer for his possession.

On the date of practical completion, two things happen:

(i)   certain matters cease to operate;
(ii)   certain matters start to operate.

The matters which cease to operate after the date of practical completion are, amongst others, as follows:
(a)   Contractor's responsibilities for insurances;
(b)   Architect's authority to issue instructions except under clause 2.6;
(c)   daywork rates under clause 3.7.5;
(d)   price fluctuation clauses;
(e)   damage from frost;
(f)   any matters under the contract which are paid on a time-related basis;
(g)   liability for vandalism or criminal and malicious damage;
(h)   liquidated damages;
(i)   direct loss and/or expense claims;
(j)   cessation of contract rates and prices.

Those matters which only start to operate from the date of practical completion include:

(i)   full responsibility of possessing the works by the Employer;
(ii)   liability for insurance;
(iii)   liability for vandalism or criminal and malicious damage
(iv)   liability for frost damage;
(v)   revised daywork charges;
(vi)   defect liability period commences for the Contractor;
(vii)   period of final measurement commences and runs six months from the date of practical completion;
(viii) issue of final certificate should be six months from the date of practical completion;
(ix)   release of half the retention on the date of practical completion and the balance of retention at the end of the defects liability period;
(x)   should the Contractor agree to execute any additional work during the defects liability period, he should seek enhanced rates or prices or submit separate quotations;
(xi)   payment should be sought for any damage caused to the works after the date of practical completion.

The heading to the second paragraph of clause 2.1 states 'Possession by the Contractor - use or *occupation by the Employer'*. The second paragraph goes on to say *'For the purposes of the Works insurances the Contractor shall retain possession of the site and the Works up to and including the date of the issue of the Certificate of Practical Completion, and the Employer shall not be entitled to take possession of any part or parts of the Works until that date'*.

This is again the common law position but the second paragraph to clause 2.1 does make a very good point by specifically referring to the works insurances running up to the date of the practical completion certificate. Other forms of building and civil engineering contracts do, however, go one better by insisting that the works insurances continue for a further period of 14 days beyond the practical completion certificate in order to allow the Employer to effect his own insurances.

On the Appendix, at clause 6.3A.3.1, the annual renewal date of insurance supplied by the Contractor is to be stated.

The third paragraph to clause 2.1 states *'Notwithstanding the provisions of the immediately preceding paragraph, the Employer may, with the consent in writing of the Contractor, use or occupy the site or the Works or part thereof whether for the purposes of storage of his goods or otherwise before the date of Practical Completion'*. There are restrictions to the invoking of this paragraph in regard to notifying the insurers of the Employer's requirements and only if the said insurers confirm that such use or occupation will not prejudice the insurance. If the insurers agree to the use or occupation by the Employer, the Contractor's consent shall not be unreasonably withheld. The permission by the Contractor to allow the Employer the use or occupation of the works may well involve contractual claims, depending on circumstances. (Note the commentary to clause 2.9 - footnote (H) and Practice Note IFC84: IN/1, page 10.)

When the Contractor is responsible for paying the additional insurance premiums under clauses 6.3A.2 or 6.3A.3 it is a condition of confirmation from the insurers that the Contractor inform the Employer of the amount of the additional premium. The cost of the additional premium is to be added to the contract sum and the Contractor is required to provide the Employer with the receipt of the insurers for the additional premium.

Clause 2.2 - Deferment of possession

Clause 2.2 is very innovative in contrast to the other JCT standard forms, since it permits a diversion from a fundamental point of common law in so far as the contractual need for possession of the site being given on the date of possession stated in the Appendix can be waived by the Contractor for a period up to six weeks if so requested by the Employer and agreement is obtained from the insurers. (Note the reference in the Appendix to clauses 2.2, 2.4.14 and 4.11(a).)

It will be observed that clause 2.2 is an optional clause which may be implemented by means of completing the Appendix as to whether *'clause 2.2 applies/does not apply'*. A period less than six weeks may be inserted into the Appendix if so desired.

The normal common law situation which occurs when the Employer fails to give possession of the site on the date stated in the Appendix - a fundamental breach of contract going to the very root of the contract - is therefore waived under clause 2.2 for a period up to six weeks.

However, by virtue of clause 2.4.14, the Contractor is entitled to an extension of time for the period of deferment and also for direct loss and/or expense caused by prolongation. The Contractor should understand that if clause 2.2 is invoked, he loses his common law right to rescission. This is a new and important contractual claim for prolongation, because of the late start to the contract.

Clause 2.3 - Extension of time

The contractual demands given in clause 2.1 of a date for possession of the site and for the Contractor thereupon to begin and regularly and diligently proceed with the works and to complete the same on or before the date for completion, means that the Employer, in order to retain his right to liquidated damages (amongst other things), should he or his agents delay the works by variations, daywork, failure to provide information on time or for any of the events in clauses 2.4.1 to 2.4.14, must grant suitable extensions of time. It is not legally responsible to urge the Contractor on one hand to proceed regularly and diligently and then cause delay and disruption to his progress. That is why the contract contains clause 2.3, which sets out the grounds (events) acceptable for the granting of extensions of time. Clause 2.3 gives in detail the contractual machinery for the Contractor to use in seeking to obtain an extension of time. (Note the commentary to clause 2.1 concerning the completion date and the date of practical completion.)

Clause 2.3 is a very important clause for the Contractor to grasp fully and understand and apply successfully in his own interest.

At the very best any extension of time granted obtains release from liquidated damages for the period agreed and at the most the payment of claims for those events listed in clauses 4.12.1 to 4.12.7 for which extensions of time have been given and attract financial liability from the Employer. It should be realised that not all the events listed in clause 2.4.1 to 2.4.14 attract financial claims, but only those listed in clauses 4.12.1 to 4.12.7 inclusive.

If the Contractor is going to seek contractual claims he must follow strictly the contract requirements to establish these claims successfully. It is always wiser to seek a possible claim in writing, even if subsequently the Contractor actually withdraws such a claim. It is infinitely easier to withdraw a timeous claim rather than attempt to submit an out-of-time claim which will be rejected by the Employer or his agents for that reason alone.

The successful initiation of a contractual claim for an extension of time is given in clause 2.3, paragraph one, which states *'Upon it becoming reasonably apparent that the progress of the Works is being ... delayed'*. The Contractor must follow the procedure given in clause 2.3 but before examining the requirements of the clause, it should be seen that it is *'the Works'* that are visibly seen to be delayed and not *'any part thereof'*. By contrast under clause 4.11(b) in regard to a claim of direct loss or expense for disturbance of the regular progress of the works, it goes on to state *'or part thereof'* and this distinction sometimes misleads Contractors over clause 2.3, which is only concerned with delay to the works per se. Apart from the positive side of clause 2.3, which pertains to the actual works being delayed, there is also the negative side which relates to the possibility of *'or is likely to be delayed'* and which is a much more difficult case to establish or prove.

What is to be understood by the phrase *'upon it becoming reasonably apparent'* that delay has occurred? At the very minimum it must mean that it can be seen by the Employer, Architect or agents that the works are visibly delayed including the 'man in the street' or 'the man on the Clapham omnibus' or 'the reasonable man'. It cannot be a mere hypothesis but it must be a fact of the contract's life.

The decision as to whether or not an extension of time should be granted is a matter for the Architect alone. The Employer cannot interfere in the decision by attempting to veto the Architect's issue of an extension of time. A Minor Works Agreement contract went to litigation when the Employer informed the Architects that they were not to grant any further extension of time. However, the Architect granted a further extension of time and the Employer wrote to the Architect saying they should not grant any further extensions of time without his written approval. The Employer then visited the site and told the Contractor that the Architect had no power to grant extensions of time. The Judge subsequently ruled in favour of the Architect's decision. (Details given in *Building Design* February 16, 1990, page 11.)

Clause 2.3 - Paragraph 1
This requires the Contractor, when he has established that a delay has occurred, to give written notice of the cause of the delay to the Architect. The nature of the written notice to the Architect must not be just limited to clause 2.4 'events', since the Contractor should give all the reasons for delay, irrespective of whether they will give grounds for an extension of time or not. For instance, if one of the operatives on the site has a fierce argument with the site agent and kills him in a moment of intense anger, it is inevitable that delay will occur for which the Contractor is not entitled to an extension of time or payment for the disruption of the loss of morale to the operatives. Again, if the Contractor runs into a difficult time due to his inability to obtain finance, he must give the Architect details and will not be entitled to an extension of time.

Likewise, it is necessary for the Employer, the Architect and other agents to inform the Contractor of any delays of which they are aware to allow the Contractor to attempt to mitigate these circumstances. An example could be that the structural engineer learns that there will be a delay in the delivery of the structural steelwork long before the Contractor can possibly know of this fact. The judgment in the case of the *London Borough of Merton v Stanley Hugh Leach Ltd (1985)* gives valuable instruction in these important issues.

The next fundamental legal matter concerning the delay of the works, even if for events given in 2.4.1 to 2.4.14, is that such events concurrently must cause the contract to be delayed beyond the date of completion given in the Appendix. This point is often overlooked by Contractors. If delay takes place which does not warrant an extension of time it may, however, allow for a financial claim to be made under clause 4.11(b) instead.

Therefore, it will be necessary for these two concomitant or co-terminus issues to coincide at the same time, ie, the works themselves have been delayed but in addition the date for practical completion has been exceeded.

Only those grounds given in the events of clause 2.4.1 to 2.4.14 are permissible for the granting of extensions of time. Grounds other than these are not acceptable for the granting of extensions of time. The very important decision in the case of *Percy Bilton Ltd v Greater London Council (1982)* clearly establishes this.

It will be realised that this publication only deals with contractual claims and breaches of contract. Claims other than these are dealt with under the last paragraph clause 4.11 which states, *'The provisions of this clause 4.11 are without prejudice to any other rights or remedies which the Contractor may possess'*. These *'rights or remedies'* relate to arbitration or litigation. The Architect or the Quantity Surveyor are not empowered under the contract to handle these issues of *'rights or remedies'*.

Clause 2.3, paragraph one, requires the Architect, after the Contractor's submission for an extension of time by virtue of one or more of the events given in clause 2.4, as soon as he is able to estimate the length of the delay beyond the completion date given in the Appendix (or a previous extension of time already granted), make in writing a fair and reasonable extension of time for the completion of the works. (Note clause 2.5 which covers any further delay or extensions of time.) The Contractor, when he makes an application for an extension of time, should give his own evaluation of the period of time he is seeking and which event or events he has selected under clause 2.4 events. If the event allows for a financial claim under clauses 4.12.1 to 4.12.7, the Contractor should refer to this and give an estimate of the cost for the event so far and the warning that further direct loss and/or expense may follow in due time.

A very important point concerning extensions of time, which is not obviously realised by Contractors, is that should there be any ommissions from the contract, the Architect is contractually allowed to reduce any extensions of time he may consider allowable by any savings in time occasioned by those omissions. For example, if he had estimated that an extension of time could be granted of 11 weeks but that substantial savings by omissions were equal to 4 weeks, then he would be contractually correct to grant only an extension of 11-4 = 7 weeks.

Despite this principle of reducing an extension of time due to omissions, the third paragraph to clause 2.3 allows for a possible reassessment of any extensions of time already granted. The Architect may, at any time up to 12 weeks after the date of practical completion, make an extension of time in accordance with the provisions of clause 2.3, whether upon reviewing a previous decision or otherwise and whether or not the Contractor has given notice as referred to in the first paragraph hereof. The Architect cannot reduce any previously made extension of time. That is, the review can only confirm or increase an extension of time.

The Architect, by virtue of the last paragraph to clause 2.3, may request the Contractor to provide such information as is necessary for him to estimate any period for an extension of time.

Clause 2.3 - Paragraph 2

Paragraph two restricts the number of events to be considered by the Architect after the date for completion (or after the expiry of any extended time previously fixed under this clause) but before practical completion is reached.

The Architect is then required, as soon as he is able, to estimate the length of the delay, if any, to the works resulting from that event, and make in writing a fair and reasonable extension of time for the completion of the works.

The six events listed in the second paragraph to clause 2.3 are:

(i) Clause 2.4.5.
     Compliance with the Architect's instructions for clauses 1.4 (inconsistencies),3.6 (variations), 3.8 (provisional sums), 3.15 (postponement) or to the extent provided therein, under clause 3.3 (Named Sub-contractors).

(ii) Clause 2.4.6.
      Work ordered to be opened up and found to be in accordance with the contract.

(iii) Clause 2.4.7.
       The Contractor not receiving in time from the Architect necessary instructions, drawings, details or levels.

(iv) Clause 2.4.8.
      Delay by the Employer's own operatives or others.

(v) Clause 2.4.9.
     Delay or failure by the Employer to supply materials or goods on time.

(vi) Failure by the Employer to give in due time ingress or egress from the site.

These six clauses each allow the Contractor not only to claim extensions of time but also permit claims for direct loss and/or expense for possible prolongation and disruption which are the financial liabilities of the Employer.

Clause 2.4.3 can also provide for financial claims of direct loss and/or expense because of loss or damage caused by any one of the specified perils. These are met by either the insurers of the Contractor or the Employer, as dictated by the contract requirements.

Clause 2.4.14, which again permits claims for direct loss and/or expense under clause 4.11(a), relates to a deferred start to the contact and is not an extension of time claim as such but a revised starting date.

It is important to refer to Practice Note PH/IN/84 on page 4 which states *'there is also a specific provision in respect of some of those events occurring before Practical Completion when the Date for Completion has passed or after expiry of any extension of time previously given'*. This makes it clear that the Architect may extend the time for completion in respect of instructions, the need for which only becomes apparent when the progress of the works has reached a certain stage.

This does not affect the general requirement that the Contractor shall be given information to enable him to complete the works by the date for completion.

It is plain that any extension of time granted must be after the original contract date for practical completion, so the reference to a change in the date of practical completion must refer to the revised date of practical completion. The purpose of this particular power for the Architect lies in the possibility he may not have been able to make decisions concerning drawings, details, levels, instructions and the like until the Contractor has reached a specific stage in the execution of the works. (Note the Practice Note IN/1/84 reference (b) on page 2 *'Specific provision for the Architect to make in certain circumstances an extension of time after the due completion date has passed'.* The 'due' completion date relates to the completion date stated in the Appendix or a revised completion date after the granting of extensions of time under the clause 2.3.)

It is important to note that clauses 2.5, 2.6, 2.7, 2.8 and 2.9 deal with these problems in detail. (Note the commentary on these clauses.)

No variations can be given by the Architect after the issue of a practical completion certificate.

Under IFC84, an Architect may cancel any previously issued certificate of non-completion under clause 2.6 and would then have also to comply with clause 2.8.

Whether the Contractor is still required to give a written notice for paragraph two, as paragraph one requirement of clause, is not made obvious. Presumably a Contractor would make a written application in order to safeguard his financial and contractual interests.

Clause 2.3 - Paragraph 3 - Reviewing extensions of time

Paragraph three of clause 2.3 gives authority to an Architect, for a period up to 12 weeks after the date of practical completion, to make an extension of time in accordance with the provisions of clause 2.3, whether upon reviewing a previous decision or otherwise and whether or not the Contractor has given notice (in writing), as referred to in the first paragraph hereof.

However, the Architect cannot reduce the length of a previously made extension of time.

The Architect's review of extensions of time, or the granting of an extension of time, is in respect of any event at any time up to 12 weeks after the date of practical completion. (Note page 4 of the Practice Note PN/IN/1.) Whilst it is not necessary for the Contractor to have given a written notice to the Architect, it should be incumbent upon the Contractor to press home his request for an additional extension of time should he consider it important to do so and not rely on the possibility that the Architect may (might) review the contractual situation. Because the Architect cannot reduce any previous extension of time, the Contractor has nothing to lose by pressing home his arguments. Further, at the end of the day, it may well be a general review of all the circumstances of the contract may bring to light events or facts previously overlooked.

Clause 2.3 - Paragraph 4 - Mitigation

The fourth paragraph to clause 2.3 makes any claim for an extension of time subject to the legal doctrine of mitigation. The Contractor has always to use his best endeavours to prevent delay and shall do all that may be reasonably required to the satisfaction of the Architect to proceed with the works. The decision in the case of *British Westinghouse Electric & Manufacturing Co v Underground Electric Rail Company of London* (1912)(HOL) established at common law that there is an obligation by the Contractor to take all reasonable care to mitigate loss and damage. If he does not take such steps he is prevented from claiming some of his loss and damage.

Paragraph four of clause 2.3, therefore, makes the legal doctrine of mitigation an express clause in the contract, even though the doctrine could have been implied into the contract as a matter of common law. (Note the strong terminology in the fourth paragraph, *'always'* and *'shall use constantly the Contractor's best endeavours to prevent delay'*. In the case of *UBH (Mechanical Services) Ltd v Standard Life Assurance Co* it was decided that 'reasonable endeavours' was less onerous than to use 'best endeavours'. So, legally, 'best endeavours' implies a high level of application by the Contractor and must also have a high risk potential.)

Clause 2.3 - Paragraph 5

Paragraph five to clause 2.3 is mandatory in requiring the Contractor to provide such information as is required by the Architect and as is reasonable for the purposes of clause 2.3. If the Contractor fails to give the Architect the information he desires to form an opinion over an extension of time, the Architect is entitled contractually to insist on being given this information. Should the Architect be dissatisfied with the information given, he will have every right to reject the whole or part of the extension of time period sought.

The General Rule

The general rule of common law concerning building contracts which have a liquidated damages clause and an obligation by the Contractor, means that in the event of the contract over-running and there being no grounds for granting an extension of time, the Contractor must pay liquidated damages. However, the general rule was dealt with in detail by Lord Fraser in the House of Lords case of *Percy Bilton Ltd v Greater London Council* (1982) where he stated that the common law general rules may be amended by the express terms of a contract. (This is accomplished in IFC84 by clauses 2.4.1 to 2.4.14.) Without such clauses extensions of time would not be possible for those grounds (events).

Further, by the legal doctrine of the 'inclusion of one thing' in a contract means the 'exclusion of another thing'.

Clause 2.4 - Events

Paragraph one of clause 2.3 requires the Contractor to state in his application for an extension of time which event under clause 2.4 warrants an extension of time being granted.

Clause 2.4 devolves into fourteen different events which may be considered by the Architect for an extension of time. Contractually, only these events may be considered by the Architect. It is absolutely essential for the Contractor to be able to prove material facts which will establish bona fide grounds for being granted an extension of time for one or more events listed in the clause and not merely to voice an opinion as to which events apply. Each of those events listed in clauses 2.4.1 to 2.4.14 will now be considered individually.

Clause 2.4.1 - Force majeure

Force majeure is a French legal term which has been incorporated into English law. In the case of *Leabeaupin v Crispin* (1920) (HOL) their Lordships stressed the need to construe the interpretation of the phrase in close attention to the words which precede or follow it and with due regard to the nature and general terms of the contract.

In clause 2.4 the preceding words are *'the following are the events referred to in clause 3.2'*. Therefore, it follows that force majeure is a contractually acceptable ground for granting an extension of time.
 In defining force majeure, it is necessary to state that in the previous legal case, it was decided that it excluded the Contractor's own act or negligence or omission or default. War was acceptable as being within the interpretation of force majeure in *Zinc Corporation v Hirsch* (1916). Force majeure is not an 'Act of God'; nor is it 'bad weather'. This was decided in *Matsoukes v Priestman* (1915).

Government legislation becoming law after the contract had been entered into could be grounds for force majeure.

Clause 7.8.1(a) states that force majeure is a ground for the Employer or Contractor to determine his own employment under the contract, providing the carrying out of the whole of works or substantially the whole of the uncompleted works is suspended for a period of three months.

Clause 2.4.2 - Exceptionally adverse weather conditions.

The grounds for an extension of time under clause 2.4.2 is for *'exceptionally adverse weather conditions'*. This ground (event) is not very clear in itself. On average, in Southern England it rains approximately 50 mm per month and before any considerations given for a claim under this event allowance must first be made for this 50 mm of rain. Next, the weather must be exceptional as well as adverse. Further, the state of the works must be examined, since if they are entirely roofed, the roads and paths and drainage completed, the effect of exceptionally adverse weather must be very limited or not at all. The circumstances would be different if the building was at the excavation stage with deep foundations, trenches and a basement.

An exceptionally adverse aspect of the weather could be a very heavy fall of snow in June, ie, well out of the normal season.

There are two aspects to exceptionally adverse weather conditions. Firstly, the actual weather itself, eg, if torrential rain falls for seven days without a let-up in the early stages of the contract could possibly cause a delay of one week. Secondly, the rain may heavily flood the site. This is a 'condition due to weather conditions' and is a separate issue resulting from the first consideration.

Even though the rain has stopped and ceases to be exceptionally adverse, the result may be quagmire conditions and the need for pumping and disposal of storm water. Although storm, tempest and flood are issues for clause 6.3A, 6.3B or 6.3C, which deals with the insurance of the works, it is important to understand the distinction between exceptionally adverse weather conditions and the conditions on site as a result of such weather.

The contractor should, as a normal precaution, keep day-to-day records of the weather in order to prove when exceptionally adverse weather conditions caused actual delay to the works.

The contractor can obtain summaries of weather conditions from official records kept by the Meteorological Office to support his arguments. Similarly, newspaper reports and photographs of the effects of exceptional weather may prove useful.

Clause 2.4.3 - Loss or damage caused by any one or more of the specified perils
The specified perils given as grounds (events) under clause 2.4.3 are defined in clause 8.3 as:

'Fire, lightning, explosion, storm, tempest, flood, bursting or overflowing of water tanks, apparatus or pipes, earthquake, aircraft and other aerial devices or articles dropped therefrom, riot and civil commotion but excluding Excepted Risks.'

Excepted risks are also defined in clause 8.3 as follows:

'Ionising radiations or contaminated by radioactivity from any nuclear fuel or from any nuclear waste from the combustion of nuclear fuel, or other hazardous properties of any explosive nuclear assembly of nuclear component thereof, pressure waves caused by aircraft or other aerial devices travelling at sonic or supersonic speeds.'

Grounds for an extension of time under clause 2.4.3 are limited to any one or more of the specified perils and only those specific perils.

The legal phrase 'loss or damage' is most likely an abridgement of 'loss of the works' or 'damage to the works' as well as site materials as required by clauses 6.3.2, 6.3A and 6.3B. Alternatively, 'loss or damage' could be interpreted as 'destruction and damage'.

It does not matter who is responsible under the contract for the insurance of specified perils, since the Contractor is entitled to an extension of time should a specified peril occur. The Contractor is advised to make an immediate claim for an extension of time without stating how much time is sought until the whole situation is known or decided.

There are no grounds for an extension of time for criminal damage or vandalism, with the exception of arson by reason of 'fire'. Theft is not dealt with under clause 2.4.3 and, therefore, no extension of time can be granted. The cost of replacing stolen goods and materials is payable under the all risks insurance of clauses 6.3A, 6.3B and 6.3C.

In seeking to calculate an extension of time for loss or damage caused by specified perils it must be borne in mind that there may be the need for demolition of work left standing, as well has removing from the site all debris before the re-erection of the damaged work may be commenced. Damage to a building would be less than the total destruction of the works executed.

Clause 7.8.1(b) states that *'loss or damage to the Works occasioned by any one or more of the specified perils'* is a ground for the Employer or Contractor to determine his own employment under the contract, providing the carrying out of the whole of the works or substantially the whole of the uncompleted works is suspended for a period of three months. However, there is a caveat in clauses 7.8.2 which states that the Contractor shall not be entitled to give notice under clause 7.8.1 where the loss or damage to the works occasioned by one or more of the specified perils was caused by the negligence of the Contractor, his servants or agents, or by any Sub-contractor, his servants or agents.

Clause 2.4.4. - Civil commotion or strikes

Clause 2.4.4 enumerates the possibility of civil commotion or strikes of various persons concerned in the execution of the works to a lesser or greater degree, since it extends from those actually working on the site to those working off-site, as well as the transportation of goods or materials required for the works. The cause of a strike would not be permissible legally if wilfully engendered by the Contractor himself.

The case of *L.R.E. Engineering Services v Otto Simon Carves* (1981) involved a strike by others outside the perimeter of the contractual site, which effectively blocked the entrance to the site and prevented entrance by the Contractor. This was not accepted by the Judge as grounds for granting an extension of time.

Any extension of time granted under clause 2.4.4. does not commit the Employer to any financial liability for prolongation or disruption, direct loss and/or expense.

Under IFC84, civil commotion is a ground for determination by the Employer or the Contractor of his own employment under the contract.

Clause 7.8.1(c) states that *'civil commotion'* is a ground for determination under the contract, providing that the carrying out of the whole of the works, or substantially the whole of the completed works, is suspended for a period of three months.

Clause 2.4.5 - Architect's instructions

Clause 2.4.5 delineates the grounds for granting an extension of time by reason of the Architect's instructions under five clauses of the contract as follows:

(a)   inconsistencies - clause 1.4;
(b)   variations - clause 3.6;
(c)   provisional sums - clause 3.8;
(d)   postponement - clause 3.15;
(e)   Named Sub-contractors - clause 3.3.

The Contractor is entitled under clause 4.12.7 to make a contractual claim for prolongation and disturbance of the regular progress of the works when direct loss and/or expense has been incurred.

It should be realised that under the contract, the Architect does not have power to confirm any instructions given orally! The Contractor should weigh this fact very carefully, as he may well lose out if he inadvertently carried out a verbal instruction which the Architect cannot subsequently confirm.

The Contractor must, therefore, obtain a written instruction before commencing any additional work. (He should, of course, always do this in every instance.) It could also be argued against him, as a contractual fact, that he had proceeded without protesting. (Note item 3 on page 2 of Practice Note 14/1-84.)

The Contractor can determine his own employment under the contract unless caused by reason of his negligence or default or that of his servants or agents - should there be a suspension of work for a continuous period of one month in relation to clauses 1.4, 3.6 or 3.15.

Where SMM7 is used, then clause 2.4.5 in regard to clause 3.8 should be amended to conform with Amendment 4 to the standard form in regard to clause 2.4.5. Similarly, for clause 2.4.7 and for a new clause 2.4.15, which allows for an extension of time for an approximate quantity included in the contract documents which is not a reasonably accurate forecast of the work required.

Clause 2.4.6 - Opening up or the testing of work
Clause 2.4.6 pertains to the Architect's power to issue instructions requiring the opening up or the testing of any of the work, materials or goods (in accordance with clauses 3.12 or 3.13.1), including making good in consequence of such opening up or testing, unless the inspection or test showed that the work, materials or goods were not in accordance with the contract. (Note clause 3.14 in the circumstances when the work is not in accordance with the contract.)

If the opening up or testing established that items involved were in accordance with the contract, then the Contractor is entitled to claim for an extension of time, should delay have occurred to the works, and for a claim for prolongation and disturbance to the regular progress of the works for any loss and/or expense incurred thereby.

The Contractor may determine his own employment under the contract by reason of clauses 7.5.3(a) and 3.6.1 should a suspension for a continuous period of one month be issued under an Architect's instruction concerning clause 3.6.1 with regard to the removal of work executed, materials or goods in accordance with the contract.

Clause 2.4.7 - Late instructions, drawings, details or levels
Clause 2.4.7 requires the Contractor specifically to make a written application for any necessary instructions, drawings, details or levels from the Architect. If the Architect fails to supply this information on the appropriate date the Contractor is entitled to a claim for an extension of time if delay ensues. However, there are limitations to the Contractor's request for information from

the Architect by reason of the fact that the application must not be unreasonably distant from nor unreasonably close to the date upon which it was necessary for the Contractor to receive the information. This distinction of time is illustrated as follows:

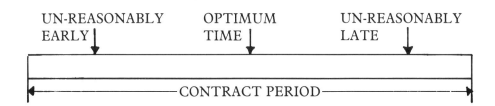

The restriction in clause 2.4.7 lies in the fact that the Contractor must judge the optimum time for requesting information. If his request is too early or too late, then it is not possible for the Architect to grant an extension of time.

On one hand, for the Contractor to write to the Architect seeking a colour schedule for the decorations to the building in the first few weeks of the contract would be far too early. On the other hand, to have fixed formwork and complicated rod reinforcement and to have ordered ready-mix concrete for delivery on a Wednesday and then to telephone the Architect late on the day before seeking information on the spacing and diameters of the reinforcement, would be far too late.

The vital key to the interpretation of clause 2.4.7 lies in the fact that the request for information *'was made on a date which having regard to the Date for Completion stated in the Appendix or any extended time then fixed'*.

If a Contractor has submitted his programme for the execution of the work, the programme shows a much shorter period for the execution of the works than that derived from the dates given in the Appendix for commencement and completion, then the relevant date for deciding whether the request for information is too early or late is that given in the Appendix and not that in the Contractor's programme. (Note the very important legal decision given in the case of *Glenlion Construction v The Guinness Trust* (1988).)

It should be realised that the dates of commencement and of completion are immutable and cannot be contractually reduced. Even if the Contractor completes before the date of completion given in the Appendix, the Employer does not have to take possession until the date of completion is reached. The Contractor is, therefore, fully liable to the Employer until that date.

With reference to the reasonableness of time in supplying requested information, the Judge in

Neodox v Borough of Swinton & Pendlebury (1958) stated that an application did not depend solely on the convenience and practical interests of the Contractor. It also depended on the engineer having time to provide it and the point of view of the Employer. (Note also a similar decision in *A. MacAlpine & Son v Transvaal Provincial Administration* (1974).)

In the case of *London Borough of Merton v Leach* (1985) the Judge considered that the issue of a correct contract programme from the Contractor was in effect an *'application in writing'* to the Architect.

Under clause 4.12.1 the Contractor may make a claim for prolongation and disturbance to the regular progress of the works. It is possible for the Contractor to determine his own employment under the contract by reason of clause 7.5.3(b), should the works be suspended for a continuous period of one month because of the Architect's failure to provide information on time.

Clause 2.4.8 - Work executed by the Employer or by others
Clause 2.4.8 contemplates delay to the works by *'the execution of work not forming part of this Contract by the Employer himself or by persons employed or otherwise engaged by the Employer ... or the failure to execute this work'.*

Therefore, the Contractor may make a claim for an extension of time should the granting of an extension of time should the delay occur by reason of the causes given in clause 2.4.8.

If the granting of an extension of time also incurs direct loss and/or expense because of prolongation and disturbance to the regular progress of the works the Contractor is entitled to a financial claim as provided for in clause 4.12.3. The Contractor may also determine his own employment under the contract should a suspension be ordered for a period of one month as provided under clause 7.5.3(c).

Clause 2.4.9 - Materials or goods supplied by the Employer
Clause 2.4.9, as distinct from clause 2.4.8 - which allows direct work by the Employer - deals with the supply of materials or goods supplied by the Employer or the failure to so supply.

Under clause 2.4.9, the Contractor is entitled to make both a claim for an extension of time as well as financial claims for loss and/or expense incurred by prolongation and disturbance to the regular progress to the works under clause 4.12.4.

Similarly to clause 2.4.8, the Contractor may determine his own employment under the contract by virtue of clause 7.5.3(c), provided a suspension has been ordered for a continuous period of a month.

Clause 2.4.10 - Delay due to inability to secure labour
Clause 2.4.10 is an alternative clause and can only exist under the contract if it has been implemented under the aegis of the Appendix which states *'clause 2.4.10 (Labour) applies/does not apply'.*

In the event of clause 2.4.10 being implemented, the Contractor is entitled to make a claim for delay caused by his inability for reasons beyond his control *'to secure such labour as is essential to the proper carrying out of the Works'*. There are three effective restrictions to operating this clause. Firstly, the grounds must not have been known or foreseen at the base date of the tender. Secondly, if it was known at this time that there was a shortage of bricklayers due to the proximity of other Contractors in the immediate area, the Contractor cannot make a claim for an extension of time due to this reason. It would be expected in these circumstance that a prudent Contractor would have made financial provision for this difficulty. Thirdly, the labour not obtainable must be essential to the works. There is no provision for a financial claim for prolongation or disturbance to the regular progress of the works.

Neither are there any grounds for the Contractor to determine his own employment under the contract by reason of a suspension on this ground.

Clause 2.4.11 - Delay due to inability to secure goods or materials

Clause 2.4.11 is an alternative clause and can only exist under the contract if it has been implemented under the aegis of the Appendix which states *'Clause 2.4.11 (Goods or Materials) applies/does not apply'*.

In the event of clause 2.4.11 being implemented the Contractor is entitled to make a claim for delay caused by his inability for reasons beyond his control to secure goods or materials which are essential to the proper carrying out of the works. There are three effective restrictions to the operation of this clause. Firstly, the grounds must not have been known or foreseen at the base date of the tender. Secondly, if it is known at this time that there is a country-wide shortage of bricks, the Contractor cannot make a claim for an extension of time for this reason. A prudent Contractor would have made provision for this problem to overcome this difficulty.

The third restriction lies in the goods or materials being essential to the proper carrying out of the works.

There is no provision for a financial claim for prolongation or disturbance to the regular progress of the works.

Neither are there any grounds for the Contractor determining his own employment under the contract by reason of suspension for this ground.

Clause 2.4.12 - Failure by the Employer to give ingress to or egress from the site

Clause 2.4.12 relates to the failure of the Employer to give, during the currency of the contract and in due time, ingress or egress from the site of the works or any part thereof, through or over any land, buildings, way or passage adjoining or connected with the site and in the possession and control of the Employer.

The clause is also linked to clause 3.6.2 which allows the Employer to impose additional obligations or restrictions or to omit any such obligations or restrictions so imposed by him in the specification, schedules of work, contract bills in regard to:

(a)   access to the site or use of any specific parts of the site;
(b)   limitations on working space (area);
(c)   limitations of working hours;
(d)   the execution or completion of the work in any specific order.

The Employer can only change those matters in clause 3.6.2 which are actually included in the contract documents. (Note the commentary to clause 3.6.2).

Clause 2.4.12 is very widely drafted and provides grounds for making a claim for an extension of time and for a claim for prolongation and disturbance to the regular progress of the works if any delay occurs under the head of clause 4.12.6.

It is envisaged that under clause 2.4.12 the Employer may have to close one or more accesses to the site, perhaps due to circumstances beyond his control. For instance if the contract is to be delayed it may be that a wayleave may lapse or be rescinded.

On the other hand, should the Employer be able to open up more access points than provided for in the contract and there is a consequent saving of time to the contract period, then the Architect is entitled to reduce any future extension of time by the period of time saved.

If the problems of access cause the Architect to issue a suspension of a continuous period of one month, then the Contractor is entitled under clause 7.5.3(d) to determine his employment.

Clause 2.4.13 - Delays by statutory authorities or statutory undertaker
Clause 2.4.13 allows the Contractor to make a claim for an extension of time should delay be caused by a local authority or statutory undertaker carrying out work in pursuance of its statutory obligations in relation to the works, or the failure to carry out such work. For example, if a cross-over is included in the contract for the local authority to execute and a delay occurs, then the Contractor may make a claim. However, if the local authority is executing any work near to or on the site which is not in connection with the contract, then any delay does not qualify for an extension of time. (Note the commentary to clause 2.4.4.)

There are no grounds for a contractual claim for prolongation or disturbance to the regular progress of the works. Neither are there any grounds for the Contractor determining his own employment.

Clause 2.4.14 - Deferment to the possession of the site
Clause 2.4.14 is only contractually applicable if clause 2.2 of the Appendix is brought into operation, ie where it states 'clause 2.2 applies/does not apply'. It is surprising that clause 2.4.14 provides grounds for an extension of time since clause 2.2 changes the date of possession to a new date (not exceeding six weeks). In these circumstances it would be expected that the revised date

of commencement would be employed and that extensions of time would run from the new date for completion for up to six weeks. (Note clause 4.11(a) in this respect.)

Nevertheless, clause 2.4.14 decides that a delay in commencement is to be treated as an extension of time. Obviously, the claim for an extension of time cannot exceed six weeks. There should not be any problem over this issue. The Architect and Employer will undoubtedly be involved in the discussions leading to the final decision of the revised date. The Contractor should make a prolongation claim under clause 4.11(a). For this event there are no grounds for the Contractor to seek to determine his employment. Presumably, if the Employer can give possession for a period greater than six weeks, then the matter will have to be resolved financially between the Employer and the Contractor. It could be a very delicate matter as the legal doctrine of rescission must inevitably overshadow any discussions.

Some grounds not acceptable for the granting of an extension of time are:

- vandalism;
- damage, malicious damage or criminal damage;
- arson by the Contractor;
- theft;
- writs issued by others compelling the Contractor to curtail noise and the consequences thereby of reducing working hours;
- strikes by domestic Sub-contractors or suppliers due to the fault of the Contractor;
- strikes outside the perimeter of the site by others preventing access;
- clause 6 perils, other than specified perils (clause 8.3);
- compliance with Acts of Parliament ruling at the time of tender;
- any matter not given in clause 2.4;
- insolvency of domestic Sub-contractors or suppliers;
- interference by gypsies;
- interference by squatters;
- trespass by others not 'invitees' to the site;
- Contractor's variations not instructed by the Architect;
- Contractor using better labour and materials than actually specified under the contract;
- instructions issued by the Architect with regard to the removal of any work, materials or goods not in accordance with the contract;
- damage to pipes and cables and the like;
- air trespass writs due to the Contractor's cranes;
- any exercise after the date of tender by the U.K. Government or any statutory power which directly affects the execution of the works by restricting the availability or use of labour which is essential to the proper carrying out of the works, or preventing the Contractor from, or delaying the Contractor in, securing such goods or materials or such fuel or energy as are essential to the proper carrying out of the works unless force majeure;
- if either clauses 2.4.9 or 2.4.10 or both do not apply by failing to be incorporated in the Appendix, then extensions of time cannot be granted;
- discovery of fossils or antiquities.

Clause 2.4.15 - Approximate quantity

If SMM7 is to be used, then an additional clause is required under Amendment 4. Clause 2.4.15 states *'by reason of the execution of work for which an approximate quantity is included in the Contract Documents which is not a reasonably accurate forecast of the quantity of work required'*.

General observations relating to clause 2.4

The importance of giving a written notice for any extension of time to which the Contractor believes he is entitled cannot be overstressed. In the case of *Twickenham Garden Developments v Hounslow Borough Council* (1970) the Judge stated that a 'notice' has a continuing effect. He also stated that a 'notice' is a warning and 'loads the pistol' but unless something else occurs the pistol cannot be discharged. It is far better to have wisely loaded the pistol rather than foolishly fire the pistol without a bullet.

The granting of extensions of time by the Architect, whether with financial liability or not, is the most basic principle for initiating and originating contractual claims. The granting of extensions of time must establish first and foremost that there has been a delay to the works and a release of the liability for liquidated damages at the very least. The two largest amounts in a contractual claim are often the loss and/or expense of prolongation and disturbance to the regular progress of the works.

Clause 2.5 - Further delay or extension of time

Clause 2.5 is a 'sweeping up' or 'catch all' clause in that it states *'in clauses 2.3 (Extension of time), 2.6 (Certificate of non-completion) and 2.8 (Repayment of liquidated damages), any references to delay, notice or extension of time or certificate include further delay, further notice, further extension of time or further certificate as appropriate'*. Clause 2.5 provides an interpretation of the verb intransitive 'delay', which also presumably gives a wider meaning to the various words used throughout the clause.

Clause 2.6 - Certificate of non-completion

Should the Contractor fail to complete the works by the date of completion, or within any extended time fixed under clause 2.3, then the Architect, under clause 2.6, must issue a certificate to that effect in order that liquidated damages may be deducted by the Employer.

The legal significance of a certificate means that it has 'form, substance and intent' as was pleaded in the case of *Token Construction v Charlton Estates* (1973), which also referred to the case of *Minister Trust v Traps Tractors* (1954).

A certificate is a statement in writing by a person of official status (such as an Architect under the contract) concerning some matter within his knowledge. Another definition of a certificate in regard to building contracts is the precise operation of the opinion, judgment or skill of the Architect in respect of issues provided for under the terms of the contract. (Note the commentary to clause 1.9.)

The certificate does not have to be a pro-forma as issued by RIBA Publications Ltd and a letter is equally as good, providing the word 'certificate' is included in the text. Without the word 'certificate' being included,it will not be held legally as a certificate. The provenance for this is found in the case of *Token Construction Ltd v Charlton Estates Ltd* (1973)(CA).

The certificate, as required in the first paragraph of clause 2.6, must state the date on which the works should be completed. If no extensions of time are to be granted then the date must be the original date for completion. If extensions are to be granted then the date must be the original date for completion. If extensions of time have been granted and the works are still not completed, then the date of the last extension of time must be the date when the works should have been completed.

The second paragraph of clause 2.6 allows for a revision to the date of non-completion by permitting the Architect to cancel the previous certificate. He may issue a further certificate under the clause as necessary. This would correct any error previously made by the Architect and also allow him to issue a further extension of time if needed. The other aspect of clause 2.6 is linked to clause 2.3, paragraph two, where contractual authority is given to the Architect to issue variations after the date for completion (or after the expiry of any extensions of time previously granted). Such variations are limited to issues under clauses 2.4.5, 2.4.6, 2.4.7, 2.4.8, 2.4.9 or 2.4.12.

This view is confirmed on page 4 of Practice Note/IN/1-84 which states, '*there is specific provision in respect of those events occurring before practical completion when the date for completion has passed or after the expiry of any extension previously given*'. This makes it clear that the Architect may extend the time for completion in respect of instructions, the need for which only becomes apparent when the progress of the works has reached a certain stage. This does not affect the general requirement that the Contractor shall be given information to enable him to complete the works by the date for completion. Clause 2.6 second paragraph also correlates to clause 2.8.

Before the actual certificate of non-completion is issued the Contractor should have made very strong representations concerning his position in relation to the delays to the works so as to avoid the payment of any liquidated damages. In the judgment to the case of *Token Construction Co., Ltd. v Charlton Estates, Ltd* (1973)(CA) the Court specifically stated '*the Architect cannot certify for delay (ie non-completion) - until he has first adjudicated upon the Contractor's applications for extension of time.*'

Clause 2.7 - Liquidated damages for non-completion

Clause 2.7 makes it abundantly clear that liquidated damages can only be deducted when a certificate for non-completion has been issued by the Architect under clause 2.6. The issue of a clause 2.6 certificate may be made up to and before the issue of the final certificate under clauses 4.6 and 4.7, but not after the issue. Liquidated damages under clause 2.7 may be deducted for the period between the date of completion or extended time until the date when practical completion takes place. The rate of liquidated damages is to be given in the Appendix at clause 2.7 and will be at £x per week or any part of a week. A part of a week is counted in days since a day is considered to be the minimum time period recognised at common law. (A day is legally defined as a period of twenty-four house commencing at midnight and is indivisible, because a day is the minimum time scale recognised at law.)

If the period was 17 weeks and 6 days the total cost would be £x multiplied by 17.857 weeks, providing the contract stated £x per week or part of a week. However, if the contract stated £x per week then a part of a week such as 6 days could not be deducted legally.

The Employer, under clause 2.7, may deduct the total value of the liquidated damages from any monies due or to become due to the Contractor (including any balance stated as due to the Contractor in the final certificate for payment) or he may recover the same from the Contractor as a debt. This means that if the liquidated damages are greater than the monies due and the Contractor refuses to pay the difference to the Employer, then the Employer is free to sue for the balance outstanding in the Courts.

In the case of *Rosehaugh Stanhope (Broadgate Phase 6) PLC and Another v Redpath Dorman Long Ltd* (1990) (CA) it was decided that '*where Contractors had bona fide claims to a contractual entitlement to extensions of time to complete building works the Employers could not obtain summary judgments against them for loss and damage caused by delay until a firm and reasonable time for completion had been ascertained*'. Figure 3.1 gives three possible cases concerning the payment or avoidance of liquidated damages.

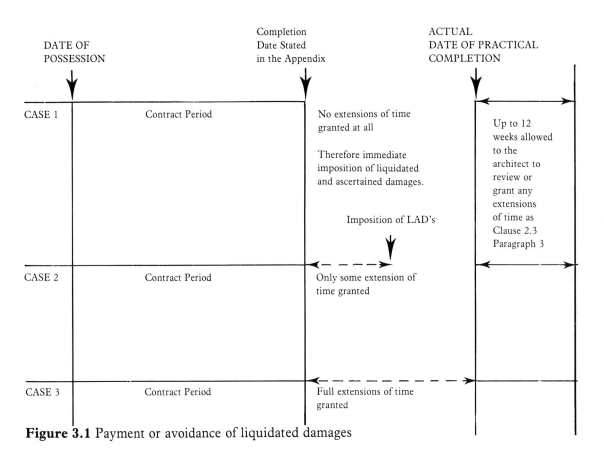

Figure 3.1 Payment or avoidance of liquidated damages

Clause 2.8 - Repayment of liquidated damages

Clause 2.8 is most important to the Contractor since should liquidated damages have been deducted under clauses 2.6 and 2.7 and the Contractor has subsequently been able to persuade the Architect that he is entitled to a further extension of time, then the original clause 2.6 certificate must be cancelled and any liquidated damages must be repaid. It is still possible, under clause 2.8, for the Architect to issue a further certificate of non-completion under clause 2.6, whereby a deduction by the Employer of other liquidated damages will be possible. The contract is absolutely clear that only the amount of the liquidated damages is to be repaid to the Contractor and no reference is made to the payment of interest on the repayment.

If the Contractor believes the value of the liquidated damages is incorrect the best time to dispute it is before signing the contract, where he may have some influence. To challenge the liquidated damages in the Courts at the end of the contract may be very difficult indeed. The Employer has the right not to press for liquidated damages but to sue for unliquidated damages, which could be far worse financially for the Contractor. The judgment of the Court of Appeal in the case of *Rapid Housing Group Ltd v Ealing Family Housing Association Ltd* is well worth studying in regard to the problem of liquidated damages and non-liquidated damages.

Clause 2.9 - Practical completion

Clause 2.9 gives authority to the Architect to issue a certificate when, in his opinion, practical completion has been achieved. The Architect has to state in his certificate the date when practical completion actually took place.

Practical completion does not mean contractually that everything has been completely finished but rather that the works have been practically completed. It is usual in these circumstances to state on the certificate of practical completion those items which still need to be completed.

There is a footnote (h) to clause 2.9 which states *'if possession is required for partial possession before practical completion, see Practice Note IH1'*. The Practice Note states that a clause 2.11 may be incorporated into the contract as follows:

'Partial Possession by the Employer

2.11   If at any time before Practical Completion of the Works the Employer with the consent of the Contract shall take possession of any part or parts of the same (any such part being referred to in this clause 2.11 as "the relevant part") then notwithstanding anything expressed or implied elsewhere in this Contract:

- *for the purpose of clause 2.10 (Defects Liability) and 4.3 (Interim payment) Practical Completion of the relevant part shall be deemed to have occurred and the defects liability period in respect of the relevant part shall be deemed to have commenced on the date on which the Employer shall have taken possession thereof;*
- *as from the date which the Employer shall have taken possession of the relevant part, the obligation of the Contractor to insure under clause 6.3A, if applicable, shall terminate in respect*

of the relevant part but not further or otherwise;

- in lieu of any sum to be paid or allowed by the Contractor under clause 2.7 (Liquidated damages) in respect of any period during which the Employer shall have taken possession of the relevant part there shall be paid or allowed such sum as bears the same ratio to the sum which would be paid or allowed apart from the provisions of this clause 2.11 as the Contract Sum, less the amount contained therein in respect of the said relevant part, bears to the Contract Sum.'

In the case of *English Industrial Estates v George Wimpey* (1973) (CA) it was decided that the Employer takes possession of any part or parts of the works only when the relevant part or parts are both handed over to him by the Contractor and is also at the same time accepted by him.

Using and occupying the part or parts of the works is not sufficient in itself to constitute taking possession.

Clause 2.10 - Defects liability
As soon as the date of practical completion is reached the defects liability period commences, ie from the day named in the certificate of practical completion. The duration of the defects liability period will be six months unless a differing period is inserted into the Appendix against clause 2.10.

However, it is quite usual to make any heating and ventilation installations, and often the electrical installation, subject to a 12 months' maintenance period. If this decision is made, then the details should be inserted into the Appendix against clause 2.10.

The final list of any defects, shrinkages or other faults are to be notified by the Architect to the Contractor not later than 14 days after the expiry of the defects liability period. However, at the end of the defects liability period the Contractor is still liable for six years under a plain contract and 12 years under a sealed contract for latent defects. Over and above these legal documents there is now the Latent Damage Act 1986 which could involve a Contractor in up to a possible five or even 16 years' liability.

The cause of defects, shrinkages or other faults must be due to materials or workmanship not in accordance with the contact or frost occurring before practical completion. One surprising omission from this category of items are goods which can also show defects, shrinkages or other faults. It is a precept of legal interpretation that a change of word indicates a change of meaning. (Note the legal decision in *R v Battle* (1870.) Therefore, the three words defects, shrinkages or other faults indicate three distinct and separate legal items.

Defects must include inferior (non-contractual) materials and/or workmanship. Shrinkages must be those shrinkages which are greater than the tolerances given or allowed for in the contract document. There will always be shrinkages, some of which will be acceptable if within the tolerances given.

Other faults could be wrong sizes, wrong positioning, wrong materials, wrong goods or those resulting from the interaction of frost on setting materials.

It is important for the Contractor to realise that the observance of an alleged 'defect' or 'fault' may only be a symptom of the real defect or fault. For example, water may be observed trickling down a basement wall. Under clause 3.12, the Architect may order the Contractor to open up for inspection that section of the basement wall which has water trickling down. On opening up the work it may be discovered that whilst generally there may be vertical asphalt tanking to the outer wall of the basement, in the area involved it may be that a portion of the asphalt tanking is defective or even missing and now requires immediate correction and remedy. By contrast it may have been the Architect who failed to specify the correct number of asphalt coats to prevent water penetration.

Clause 2.10 goes on to state that the Contractor shall make good such defects, shrinkages and other faults at no cost to the Employer. This clause has a caveat to the effect that the Architect, with the consent of the Employer, can instruct the Contractor not to make good in lieu of which he shall agree an appropriate deduction. This is an innovation in the JCT standard forms.

Clause 7.8.1 which concerns the determination by Employer or Contractor of their employment under the contract excludes 'other than the execution of work required under clause 2.10 (defects liability)'.

The operation of clause 2.10 may also invoke clauses 3.12, 3.13.1, 3.13.2 and 3.14.

The second paragraph to clause 2.10 requires the Architect, when in his opinion the Contractor's obligations under clause have been discharged, to issue a certificate to that effect.

Clause 2.10 must not mislead the Contractor into believing that only in the period of the defects liability can the Architect require the making good of defects, shrinkages or other faults. The Architect can call for the making good of these items at any time during the currency of the contract. This is clearly established, amongst others, in the cases of *AMF International Ltd v Magnet Bowling Ltd* (1968) or *Kaye (P & M) v Hosier & Dickinson* (1972)(HOL).

CONDITION 3 - CONTROL OF THE WORKS

Clause 3.1 - Assignment
Clause 3.1 sets out the contractual requirement that *'neither the Employer nor the Contractor shall, without the written consent of the other, assign this Contract'*.

This prohibition of assignment is also the common law situation. Assignment must, of necessity, arise from time to time, especially when one of the contracting parties is facing the prospect of having to cease trading or even insolvency. Another firm may wish to step in and take over the legal and financial liabilities of the contracting party which is in difficulties. In these circumstances one party to the contract may be willing to allow for an assignment, providing it is in writing and in every way financially secure and contractually competent.

Failure to obtain an agreement in writing to assign a contract can be disastrous financially.

In the case of *Helstan Securities Ltd v Hertfordshire County Council* (1978) the Contractor got into financial difficulties and without obtaining the Council's consent, assigned to the Helston Securities Ltd the amount alleged to be owing by the Council. Helston Securities Ltd brought an action against the Council and lost, because among other legal issues the Contractor could not validly assign the contract without the Council's consent. This case was under the 5th Edition of the ICE Conditions of Contract but clause 3 of that contract is very similar to the wording of clause 3.1 of IFC84.

The contract does not deal with the legal doctrine of novation which occurs (without the written permission of the Employer) when one company is totally taken over by another company, thereby absorbing all its legal and financial obligations. This then becomes a fait accompli. In other words novation involves the substitution of one of the two parties to a contract with another new party. Novation is clearly distinguishable from assignment and is most certainly irrevocable.

Clause 3.2 - Sub-contracting
Under clause 3.2 the Contractor is not allowed to sub-contract any part of the works, other than in accordance with clause 3.3, unless he has obtained the written consent of the Architect - whose consent shall not be reasonably withheld. To sub-let work without the Architect's prior consent is a serious breach of contract since it is grounds for the Employer to determine the Contractor's employment. The reason that the Architect's consent shall not be unreasonably withheld lies in the fact that the Contractor may not carry out all the trades involved in a contract and expertise is required from Sub-contractors. This is especially so today. Some Councils insert into the contract a clause calling on the Contractor to pay damages, for example of £250, every time he sub-contracts without permission.

Whilst clause 3.2 is more often honoured in its breach than its observance, the result of such a breach can be financially very serious indeed as may be witnessed in the case of *Ferguson v Welsh and Others* (1987)(HOL). That case, whilst the contract sum was only £330 for the demolition of a property, went to the Court of Appeal and then on to the House of Lords - where the Contractor lost the day!

The last paragraph to clause 3.2 states that *'it shall be a condition in any sub-contract that'* and then clause 3.2.1 follows which states in effect that in the event of the Contractor's own employment under the contract being determined (for any reason), then the employment of the Sub-contractor shall be determined immediately.

In the case of *Williams v Roffrey Bros and Nicholls (Contractors) Ltd* (1990)(CA) it was decided that *'Where one party to a contract (a Sub-contractor) valued at £20,000 agreed, in the absence of economic duress or fraud, to make a payment to the other party to the contract over and above the contract price in order to secure completion of the contract by the other party on time and thereby obtained a benefit, such as the avoidance of liquidated damages payable to a third party if the contract was not completed on time, the obtaining of that benefit to consideration for the payment of the additional sum'*. Therefore, the advantages which, from a pragmatic point of view, the Contractor hoped to obtain by agreeing to make the additional amount of £10,300 to the Sub-contractor to avoid liquidated damages or having to engage another Sub-contractor, amounted to consideration for the extra payment even though the Sub-contractor was not undertaken to do so. Therefore, the Sub-contractor was entitled to the entire payment. The Contractor lost his case. It was agreed during the course of the hearing that the Sub-contractor's tender of £20,000 was too low.

Clause 3.2.2 makes clear to the Contractor that in regard to the sub-contract:

(i)   unfixed materials or goods delivered to site must not be removed without the Contractor's written permission (clause 3.2.2(a));
(ii)   when interim payments are made, the materials or goods become the property of the Employer (clause 3.2.2(b));
(iii) when payment is made to the Sub-contractor for any such materials and goods for which the Contractor has not as yet received an interim payment from the Employer, the materials and goods become the property of the Contractor (clause 3.2.2(c));
(iv)   the operation of sub-clauses (a) to (c) of clause 3.2.2 shall be without prejudice to any property in any materials or goods passing to the Employer as provided in clause 1.11 (off-site materials or goods) of the main contract conditions.

These clauses seek to deal with the problem which arose in the case of *Dawber Williamson Ltd v Humberside County Council* (1979).

Clause 3.3 - Named persons as Sub-contractors

Clauses 3.3.1 - 3.3.8 deal with a new procedure for sub-contracting by Named Sub-contractors. Clause 3.3.1 is cross-referenced to Recital 1 with the attendant footnote (c). The footnote states *'Delete if no items specifying a named person are included in the documents'*. The relevant paragraph from Recital 1 states, *'and in respect of any work described and set out therein for pricing by the Contractor and for the execution of which the Contractor is required to employ a named person as Sub-contractor in accordance with clause 3.3.1 of the Conditions annexed hereto, has provided all of the particulars of the tender of the named person for that work in a Form of Tender and Agreement NAM/T with sections I and II completed with the Numbered Documents referred to therein'*.

If this paragraph to Recital 1 is deleted, clauses 3.3.1 to 3.3.8 inclusive cannot be used by the Architect.

Similarly, the Architect cannot give an instruction as to the expenditure of a provisional sum included in the specification, schedules of work or contract bills if the last paragraph to Recital 1 is deleted.

It has been suggested that instead of 'Named Sub-Contractors', it might well be better to refer to 'Approved Specialist Domestic Sub-Contractor', which may be considered to be more descriptive.

Clauses 3.3.1 to 3.3.8 are made applicable by invoking the last paragraph to Recital 1 making provision for work which, although it is priced by the Main Contractor, is intended to be executed or carried out by a person NAMED in the specification, schedules of work or contract bills as a (domestic) Sub-contractor using the prescribed JCT Form of Tender and Agreement NAM/T.

If the Architect wishes to invoke the use of a provisional sum for a named person, then the provisional sum must make it absolutely clear that it is for a named person and not for the Main Contractor. In the event of a provisional sum being used in the contract, the Employer pays to the Contractor an amount for the execution of the work by the named person, which is either agreed between the Employer and the Contractor or determined by the Quantity Surveyor as being a fair valuation under clause 3.7. (Note pages 7 and 8 of Practice Note/IN/1-84 as well as Practice Note 20, page 8, concerning IFC84.)

The Employer may determine the employment of the Contractor under clause 7.1(d) if he fails to comply with the provisions of clause 3.3. (named persons).

Clauses 3.3.1 to 3.3.7 inclusive shall not apply to the execution part of the works by a local authority or a statutory undertaker executing such work solely in pursuance of its statutory rights or obligations.

The usual class of work to be performed by Named Sub-contractors could include mechanical, ventilation and heating installations, electrical installations, lifts and escalators, internal telephone installations, fire alarms and sprinkler installations.

Clause 3.4 - Contractor's person-in-charge
Under clause 3.4 the Contractor is at all reasonable times to keep upon the works a competent person-in-charge. The words *'reasonable times'* is markedly different to JCT80, which calls for a competent person-in-charge to be constantly upon the works (clause 10). Clause 3.4 could mean that the competent person-in-charge is only present on a part-time basis for certain periods of the contract period and this could cause problems over prolongation direct loss and/or expense as to whether the competent person-in-charge was on site or not, as well as any problems which arise in his absence.

Clause 3.4 allows any written instructions given to the competent person-in-charge by the Architect to be deemed to have been issued to the Contractor (providing he is actually on the site at the relevant time!).

Clause 3.5 - Architect's instructions
Clause 3.5.1 provides for two distinct types of instruction, ie, instructions generally and those which require a variation under clause 3.6.2. Generally, issued instructions must be complied with by the Contractor forthwith, but with the caveat that the Architect must be empowered under the conditions to issue them. Variations under clause 3.6.2 are concerned with the imposition by the Employer of any obligations or restrictions or the addition to or alteration or omission of any such obligations or restrictions so imposed by the Employer in the specification, schedules of work or contract bills in regard to:

(a) access to the site or use of any specified parts of the site;
(b) limitations of working space (area);
(c) limitation of working hours;
(d) the execution or completion of the work in any specified order.

The saving clause 3.5.1 allows the Contractor, in respect of clause 3.6.2 variations, to make a reasonable objection in writing to the Architect. If this is accepted by the Architect the Contractor need not comply.

Clause 3.5.1 instructions by the Architect must always be in writing.

The Architect can only vary those issues in clause 3.6.2 which are in the contract documents. Therefore, the Employer cannot unilaterally impose obligations or restrictions upon the Contractor nolens volens. It is possible, if there were no limits placed on clause 3.6.2 variations, to have a change of contract which would seriously conflict with the nature and style of the contract. Changes within a contract are legally permissible but not changes of contract.

The general instructions issued by the Architect, if not complied with forthwith, are subject to the terms of the second paragraph to clause 3.5.1.

It allows for the Architect to send a written notice to the Contractor requiring compliance with an instruction. If the Contractor does not comply therewith within seven days, then the Employer may employ and pay other persons to execute such work whatsoever, which may be necessary to give effect to the Architect's instruction. All costs incurred thereby may be deducted by the Employer from any monies due to or to become due to the Contractor under the contract, or shall be recoverable from the Contractor as a debt.

Whilst clause 3.5.1 refers to the debt being deducted under 'this contract', many Employers alter the clause to read *'under this or any other contract with the Employer'*.

A possible defence to the second paragraph to clause 3.5.1 is if the Contractor claims that he is not satisfied that the Architect is empowered by the conditions to issue such an instruction.

Immediate arbitration in this instance would be possible under Article 5.1 - settlement of disputes.

If the Contractor is determined to go to immediate arbitration over a challenge to the Architect's powers to issue an instruction, the Architect may well welcome arbitration as the lesser of two evils because the Architect will be bound solely by the arbitrator's decision and not held to blame for his own decision, as would be the case if he decided not to go to arbitration.

Clause 3.5.2 develops the procedure alluded to in paragraph one of clause 3.5.1. On receipt of what purports to be an instruction issued to the Contractor by the Architect, the Contractor may request the Architect to specify in writing the provision under the Conditions which empowers the issue of the instruction. The Architect is required to comply forthwith with such a request.

If the Contractor is satisfied with the Architect's compliance to his request that is the end of the matter. This is a very important point for the Contractor to grasp because compliance means that if the instruction involves a variation order, he will receive an adjustment to the contract sum and no arbitration can now take place. This is because the Architect is bound by his compliance with the Contractor's request when he gives the contract clause which empowers him to issue his instruction. However, if the Architect's instruction is for the removal of work, materials or goods, not in accordance with the contract, the Contractor may well be justified in going to arbitration if he believes his work does conform with the contract.

There are perhaps sound reasons for correlating part of the second paragraph of clause 3.5.1 with clauses 3.12, 3.13.1, 3.13.2 and 3.14.

Clause 3.6 - Variations
Clause 3.6 provides for the Architect to issue instructions:

(a) requiring a variation;
(b) sanction in writing any variation made by the Contractor otherwise than pursuant to such an instruction.

Instructions by the Architect for variations are subject to clause 3.5.1, which, among other matters, allows the Contractor to refuse a variation under clause 3.6.2, providing he can make a reasonable objection in writing to the Architect. Apart from this objection, the Contractor must forthwith comply with the Architect's instructions or suffer the consequences of paragraph two to clause 3.5.1. (Note the commentary to clauses 3.5.1 and 3.6.2.)

The reference to the Architect sanctioning a Contractor's variation is linked to the principles involved in clauses 5.1 to 5.4.3, such as the compulsory compliance with any statute, statutory instrument, value, order, regulation, divergences or bye-law, as well as complying with all emergencies. Obviously, the Contractor cannot expect to be paid for any variations he makes to suit himself financially. He cannot, of his own free will and volition, employ far better labour and materials than specified in the contract and expect to be paid by invoking clause 3.6.

The last sentence to clause 3.6 states that *'no such instruction or sanction shall vitiate the Contract'.* It is not carte blanche to issue any variation whatever its compass. The Architect can only issue variations within the orbit of the contract itself. It was pointed out in the commentary to Recital 1 that the definition of the 'works' can in itself be very limiting. For instance, if the contract definition of the works is solely a residential property, the Architect cannot contractually issue a variation for a swimming pool or tennis courts as this is beyond the definition of the works. Of course, if it suits the Contractor he may decide to accept the variation but it is the Contractor's decision not the Architect's. The Architect is permitted to make 'changes in a contract' but he cannot make a change of contract as this would be ultra vires.

The second paragraph to clause 3.6 states *'The term Variation as used in these conditions means:'* under clauses 3.6.1 and 3.6.2 definitions are given. The definition is very wide in scope and the principles of valuation given in clauses 3.7 to 3.7.9 inclusive make it reasonably certain the Contractor should not lose out over the execution of variations.

The clause 3.6.1 definition of variations is:

'The alteration or modification of the design which in turn may change:

(a) *the quality or*
(b) *the quantity of works as shown upon the contract drawings and described by or referred to in the specification, schedules of work or contract bills including the*
(c) *addition or*
(d) *omission or*
(e) *substitution of any work*
(f) *the alteration of the kind or standard of any materials or goods to be used in the works*
(g) *the removal from the site of any work executed or materials or goods brought thereon by the Contractor for the purposes of the works, other than work, materials or goods which are not in accordance with this contract.'*

The legal phrase *'substitution of work'* seems obscure because if a brick wall is omitted and changed to a reinforced concrete wall, one both omits from and adds to the contract sum for these reasons, and effectively one type of wall has been substituted for another. Therefore, it seems almost unnecessary to invoke 'substitution' as a third alternative but, of course, if the brick wall was built and then demolished and then a reinforced concrete wall is built one wall has been substituted for another.

The removal from the site of work executed, materials or goods in accordance with the contract, no doubt relates to some extent to work thought by the Architect not to be in accordance with the contract (ie under clause 3.12) but subsequently to be completely in accordance with the contract. The Contractor is then contractually entitled to be paid for demolishing the work and then re-executing the work again by the issue of a variation under clause 3.6.1.

An example of this nature of variation may be where the Architect is led to believe that the Contractor has failed to place a horizontal layer of steel fabric reinforcement in a concrete bed over the area of the building. Subsequently, when areas of the concrete bed are opened up the correct weight of steel fabric reinforcement is found correctly placed in the middle third of the concrete bed. The Architect is then in error and the Contractor is entitled to be paid for the cost of breaking up, removing from the site the debris arising and the re-execution of the work.

The variations defined in clause 3.6.2 relate to the imposition by the Employer of any obligations or restrictions or the addition to or alteration of omission of any such obligations or restrictions so imposed or imposed by the Employer in the specification, schedules of work or contract bills in regard to:

(a) access to the site or use of any specified parts of the site;

(b)   limitations of working space (area);

(c)   limitations of working hours;

(d)   the execution of completion of the work in any specified order.

The more usual basis of determining any obligations or restrictions required by the Employer is to refer to the SMM.

Clause B.8 of SMM6 states:

'B.8 Obligations and restrictions imposed by the Employer

1.   *Particulars shall be given of any obligations or restrictions to be imposed by the Employer in respect of the following, unless they are covered by the schedules given in accordance with clause B.4.*

a.   *Access to and possession or use of the site.*

b.   *Limitations of working space (area).*

c.   *Limitations of working hours.*

d.   *The use or disposal of any materials found on site.*

e.   *Hoardings, fences, screens, temporary roofs, temporary name boards and advertising rights.*

f.   *The maintenance of existing live drainage, water, gas and other mains or power services on or over the site.*

g.   *The execution or completion of the work in any specific order or in sections or phases.*

h.   *Maintenance of specific temperature and humidity levels. Alternatively a provisional or prime cost sum shall be given.*

j.   *Temporary accommodation and facilities for the use of the Employer including heating, lighting, furnishing and attendance.*

k.   *The installation of telephones for the use of the Employer and the cost of his telephone calls shall be given as a provisional sum.*

l.   *Any other obligation or restriction.'*

Whilst SMM6 contemplates a wide range of obligations and restrictions which may be imposed by the Employer upon the Contractor, only those actually and expressly stated in the specification, schedules of work or contract bills can be the subject of a variation under clause 3.6.2. No obligations or restrictions can be imposed upon the Contractor by contract drawings since they are not included in the list of contract documents in clause 3.6.2.

If there are no obligations or restrictions given in the contract, then none can be imposed by a variation issued by the Architect.

Limitation of working hours

An example of the working hours being changed could arise in the renovation to an hotel which continues to operate during the works. Usually, the Employer requires substantial liquidated damages in the default of the Contractor to keep to the contract period. The liquidated damages are normally based on £x per bedroom, which is the main source of the Employer's income. Imagine that whilst the Contractor is working 60 hours per man per week, there is a very orientated trades union operative in the employ of the hotel who objects to the long hours the Contractor is working and threatens a strike of all hotel staff unless the Contractor reduces the working hours of his employees down to 45 hours. It is almost certain that the Employer would be forced to accept the reduction in working hours and would request the Architect to issue a variation under clause 3.6.2 limiting the hours to 45 hours per employee per week.

The requirements of SMM7 in regard to the obligations and restrictions which the Employer might require are much more specific and covers a wider scope of limitations than SMM6 under clauses A34, 35, 36, 42, 43, 44 and 50.

Limitations of working space (area)
The limitations to working space (area) could mean that the area allocated on the contract drawings for the sole use of the Contractor has, due to circumstances beyond the control of the Employer, to be reduced or curtailed. The Employer must then inform the Architect and request him to issue a variation to reduce the working space (area).

On the other hand it may be possible for the Employer to provide, during the currency of the contract, more accesses than those given on the contract drawings, and again the Architect would be required to issue a variation to deal with this eventuality.

Unless the contract was one of sectional completion, with a phased order of execution or completion, the Employer would not normally be able to request that the order of execution of completion be changed to another sequence of events. Nevertheless, under clause 3.6.2 the Employer may do so by virtue of a variation issued by the Architect upon the request of the Employer. The order of events can only be changed should there have been an order of events in the original contract documents.

The reason for this limitation or restriction lies in the fact that the Contractor is entitled to receive and to hold the entire site in his possession until the completion of the contract. The Employer or his agents are not allowed to interfere contractually in any way with the performance of the Contractor. Note the decisions in *Twickenham Garden Developments v Hounslow Borough Council* (1970) and *AMF International Ltd v Magnet Bowling and Percy Trentham* (1968).

It must not be forgotten that the Contractor may make a reasonable objection in writing to any proposed variation under clause 3.6.2.

Clause 3.7 - Valuation of variations and provisional sum work
Clauses 3.7 to 3.7.9 are devoted to the valuation of variations and provisional sums. Since IFC84 is a lump sum contract the valuation of variations and provisional sums will result in additions to and omissions from the contract sum. (Note clause 4.6 in this regard as far as the procedures are concerned for the final certificate.)

Clause 3.8 requires the Architect to issue instructions concerning the expenditure of provisional sums. (Note the commentary to clause 3.8.) Clause 3.7 relates to variations being added or deducted in respect of Architect's instructions. No variation instruction means no payment or adjustment to the contract sum. The adjustment of provisional sums also requires instructions but no reference is made to them as variations. This seems quite understandable because they must be omitted entirely and perhaps only partially or wholly added back by the Architect's instructions.

Definition of provisional

In the case of *Branca v Cobarro* (1947)(CA) it was decided that the natural and ordinary meaning of 'provisional' is *'something which is going to operate until something else happens'*. In the context of this contract is would appear to mean that provisional sums are temporary until the Architect makes a permanent decision. Inevitably this means their omission from the contract sum (which may mean their total omission from the contract or an addition of a similar amount or less or greater as the Architect may require by his instructions). Clauses 2.8 and 4.7 require the Architect to ensure that any necessary effect has been given to all terms of the contract that require additions or adjustments or deductions from the contract sum. The second paragraph to clause 4.5 specifically requires the omission of all provisional sums, ie *'as finally ascertained less all provisional sums ...'*. The prerogative for the use of provisional sums is solely that of the Architect and not the Contractor.

Under clause A.8 of General Notes of SMM6 the term 'provisional sum' is defined as *'a sum provided for work or costs which cannot be entirely foreseen, defined or detailed at the time the tendering documents are issued'*. Because there is no definition of a 'provisional sum' in the contract it follows that the definition in the SMM becomes the contractual definition. The provisional sums included in the contract must state clearly the nature of the provisional sum. Unless it is for a Named Sub-contractor or a local authority or statutory undertaker, the presumption will be that the use of the provisional sums is solely for the Main Contractor.

The requirements of a provisional sum in SMM7 are given in clauses 10.2 to 10.6. There is a distinction in SMM7 between provisional sums for 'defined work' and those for 'undefined work'. Clause 10.6 states that where provisional sums are given for undefined work the Contractor will be deemed not to have made any allowance in programming, planning and pricing preliminaries. The latter issue of undefined provisional sums will allow, if incurred, for direct loss and/or expense for any prolongation and disruption. (Note clauses 3.3.1(c) and 3.3.2(a).)

Provisional or approximate quantities

There is no specific contractual requirement dealing with the question of provisional or approximate quantities should these have been provided for in the contract documents. In contrast under GC/Works/1 - Edition 2, clauses 3(4) and 39 require *'all provisional quantities to be deducted from the Contract Sum and the value of the work ordered and executed thereunder shall be ascertained as provided by the Conditions'* and goes on to state further *'that no work under provisional quantities shall be commenced without instructions in writing from the Superintending Officer.'*. Under clause 69 the same principle of omission and remeasurement is given in very similar terms.

Whilst the contract does not spell out the necessary steps to be taken, it must be accepted as a contractual procedure that all provisional or approximate quantities are to be omitted by the Architect or Quantity Surveyor as the case may be. (Note the decision in the case of *Dudley Corporation v Parsons & Morris* (1959)(CA).)

Clause A.2 of SMM6 requires *'where the extent of the work which is not known shall be described as provisional or given in a bill of approximate quantities'*. Clause 10.1 of SMM6 requires *'where work can be described and given in accordance with these rules but the quantity of work required cannot be accurately determined, an estimate of the quantity shall be given and identified as an approximate quantity.'*. Rule 10.1, of the Code of Procedure for Measurement of Building Works states *'Work which is the subject of approximate quantities shall be re-measured as executed and the appropriate adjustment effected in accordance with the contract.'*.

The colloquial adjective - provisional - has been used because it is more frequently employed in daily use than 'approximate'.

After the provisional or approximate quantities have been omitted, the Architect must issue drawings and variation instructions in order to provide for any additions to the contract sum. It may be argued that the provisional or approximate quantities need re-measurement by the Architect or Quantity Surveyor because they originally decided the quantities to be allowed in the contract documents. But that does not deal with the contractual requirements of variations. For instance any 'soft' spots in the foundations or drainage need scheduling on site, probably by the clerk of works and the Contractor's own representative. Whether or not these and other matters are included on drawings it is crystal clear that the drawings would not only require to be delivered to the Contractor but would also need a variation instruction. If this procedure is followed the Contractor ensures that he will be paid for all the additional quantities. There is no guarantee that there will actually be a Quantity Surveyor appointed to the contract and in this case a similar procedure will have to be initiated with the Architect. Failure to obtain the necessary drawings, as well as variation instructions, could mean the Contractor not obtaining his rightful payment. It must be stressed that the Contractor must always obtain written variation instructions before executing any work under the re-measurement of provisional or approximate quantities to ensure the certainty of payment. (Note the procedure specified in clause 3.7)

Clause 3.7 states surprisingly that the amount to be added or deducted from the contract sum for instruction variations or instructions on the expenditure of provisional sums may be agreed between the Employer and the Contractor prior to the Contractor complying with any such instruction.

Over issues such as 'acceleration', which are not dealt with in the contract, it would be necessary for the Employer to negotiate directly with the Contractor as they are the two contracting parties.

This general principle is unlikely to be generally invoked (apart from issues such as acceleration), since it is much more usual for the Quantity Surveyor to deal with the adjustment to the contract sum and the second part of clause 3.7 goes on to state this ie *'but if not so agreed there shall be added to or deducted from the Contract Sum an amount determined by a valuation made by the Quantity Surveyor in accordance with the following rules.'.*

It is necessary before examining the 'valuation rules' to consider clause 3.7.1 where it defines *'priced documents'*. This term is used later in clauses 3.7.2 to 3.7.8.

Clause 3.7.1 states that *'priced document'* as referred to in clauses 3.7.2 to 3.7.8 means *'where the 2nd Recital alternative 'A' applies, the Specification or the Schedules of Work as priced by the Contractor in the Contract Bills.'.*

Clause 3.7.1 then goes on to state that where alternative 'B' applies, the *'priced document'* means the contract sum analysis or the schedule of rates, prepared and priced by the Contractor.

Variation Rule 1 may be considered to be given in clause 3.7.2 which states *'omissions shall be valued in accordance with the relevant prices in the priced document.'.*

Although this rule appears perfectly clear it is subject to clause 3.7.8 which states *'if compliance with any such instructions substantially changes the conditions under which any other work is executed, then such other work shall be treated as if it had been the subject of an instruction of the Architect requiring a variation under clause 3.6 to which clause 3.7 shall apply.'.*

Clause 3.7.8 does not itself give the reason why *'the compliance with any such instructions substantially changes the conditions under which any other work is executed'*. A clue may be seen in clause 11(4)(d) of JCT63 which states *'The prices in the Contract Bills shall determine the valuation of items omitted; provided that if omissions substantially vary the conditions which any remaining items of work are carried out the prices for such remaining items shall be valued under rule (b) of this sub-clause.* Rule (b) of JCT63 states *'The said prices, where work is not of a similar character or executed under similar conditions as aforesaid, shall be the basis of prices for the same so far as may be reasonable, failing which a fair valuation thereof shall be made.'.*

The conditions which prevail after omissions allow star items and star rates to be sought by the Contractor. IFC84 does not limit clause 3.7.8 solely to omissions but must envisage differing conditions arising from additions and the need again for star items and rates. However, it seems more than likely that it will be omissions more than additions which will affect the balance of work to be carried out.

Omissions must be genuine omissions from the contract. They cannot be omitted by the Architect and given to others because they may execute the omitted work at far more favourable rates or prices than the Contractor. Note the legal decisions in the cases of *J M Reilly Ltd v Belfast Corporation* (1966)(CA), *Carr v Berriman* (1953), *North West Metropolitan Regional Hospital Board v T A Bickerton* (1970) and *Commissioner for Main Roads v Reed and Stuart* (1974).

Omissions - Examples of star items and rates

Star items are defined as those new items which arise out of variations and changes in the description or dimensions from those in the contract documents. Because star items are different to the descriptions in the contract documents they usually involve the agreement of star rates as well. It has been stated in clause 3.7.2 that omissions shall be valued in accordance with the relevant prices in the priced document. However, there are limits to clause 3.7.2. For example, assuming a contract is placed and soon after the contract is commenced it is discovered that the Employer has not purchased 100% of the land for the site but only 70%. This must mean that 30% of the site does not belong to him and any work to be executed in that area of the site must be omitted. If the value of the work to be amended amounts to 25% of the contract it cannot be just omitted bearing the requirements of clause 3.7.8 in mind. It is suggested that in such circumstances the Contractor would be entitled to retain his overheads and profit on the items omitted, ie only the net rates of the 25% of the work so omitted would be used and not the overall rates including overheads and profit. It must not be overlooked that the remaining 70% of the work may be executed under very different conditions to the original contract and star items and star rates under clause 3.7.3 could become applicable. The total omission of some of the provisional sums may also have an adverse effect on the works to be executed.

Clause 3.7.6 may also be invoked. It requires that where appropriate there may be an addition to or reduction of any relevant items of a preliminary nature. That is to say a substantial omission of over 25% in the contract sum may result in a reduction of the preliminaries and a suitable deduction will have to be made.

A distinction exists between the omissions under clause 3.7 and omissions given under clause 1.4. The former omissions are those items in the original contract sum, whilst the latter are those items which should have been in the original Contractor sum but which by error were missed out of the tender documents by the Architect, the Quantity Surveyor and any other agents of the Employer. These have to be corrected by instructions issued under clauses 1.4 and 3.7.

Omissions per se (clause 3.7.2) must not be confused with any shortfall in the contract sum. Shortfall can occur when certain quantities are over-stated in the contract sum and need reducing down to their correct quantity and probable valuation adjustments (Note the commentary to clause 3.7.3.)

Some estimators price provisional quantities net, ie overheads and profit elements are deducted from the overall rates. This may be of some merit if there are substantial omissions but must fall short financially if there are considerable additions in the remeasurement of provisional quantities. The long-term view would tend to suggest the provisional quantities are more likely to increase than decrease.

An omission of substantial quantities by reason of a variation may affect the contract rate to a greater or lesser degree. It is suggested that the correct clause to negotiate a star item star rate is by invoking clause 3.7.3 regarding *any significant change in quantity of the work set out* in the priced document. An example of this is given after the commentary to clause 3.7.3. In addition, clause 1.4 may be invoked where there is an error in description or in quantity or omission of items in the contract documents.

Valuation Rule 2 may be regarded as being given in clause 3.7.3 which states *'for work of a similar character set out in the priced document the valuation shall be consistent with the relevant values therein making due allowance for any change in the conditions under which the work is carried out and/or significant change in quantity of the work so set out.'*.

Where work is not of a similar character it is to be valued under clause 3.7.4.

The clause must consider three possible options;

(a)   work of a similar character;
(b)   work executed under changed conditions;
(c)   any significant change in the quantity of the work.

(a)   Work of a similar character
Contract rates or prices will apply to all work of a similar character to the work set out in the contract documents.

'Similar' does not equate with 'identical'. It may be best understood in the statement 'whilst human beings are similar to one another they are not identical to each other for obvious reasons'.

Chambers Twentieth Dictionary defines the noun 'character' as 'items which are of the same stamp, kind, essential feature, quality, sort or style'.

On a normal contract it would be expected that the majority of variations (ie additions) would be valued at contract rates and prices. Under Valuation Rule 2 clause 3.7.6 would also apply in that the valuation shall include, where appropriate, any addition or reduction of any relevant items of a preliminary nature.

If the Architect decided to issue a variation to change the specification from knot, prime, stop and paint two undercoats and one finishing coat of paint on joinery to knot, prime, stop and paint two undercoats and two coats of finishing paint, then a revised rate will become necessary. The revised rate would be based on the contract rate, with due allowance being made for the extra finishing coat since this is work of a similar character.

Another example could be where the contract documents have a rate for a 4 mm hardboard item which the Architect changes to a 4 mm perforated pin board. The difference of cost is solely that of the material and the revised rate would make due allowance for this, since it is work of a similar character.

Further examples could be the changing of dimensions for items of joinery of say 76 mm x 101 mm cross-section to 95 mm x 114 mm.

(b)   Work executed under changed conditions
Foundations could readily involve work executed under changed conditions, thereby initiating star

items and star rates. This would mean using original contract rates and making due allowance for the changes. One example of different conditions could be where instead of ordinary foundations, the Contractor has to execute part of the foundations in underpinning, eg there may be a need to underpin an existing stanchion base.

Another example could be the stripping out of considerable quantities of asbestos discovered during the currency of the contract. Conditions could be changed due to variations from the contract involving discomfort, inconvenience or risk, as well as additional Working Rule payments as suggested by the following list;

(a)   winter working instead of summer;
(b)   night work instead of normal day-time working;
(c)   work executed at higher or lower levels such as chimneys or tunnels, adits or sub-ways;
(d)   work executed in refrigerators or boilers;
(e)   conditions due to the discovery of high level water tables on what was believed to be a dry site;
(f)   work involving close contact with dirt, filth or contaminated material;
(g)   work involving prolonged exposure to dust or spray;
(h)   work involving furnace fire-brick and acid resisting brickwork;
(i)   work executed under compressed air conditions;
(j)   work involving the use of swings, cradles, boats or boatswains chairs;
(k)   work involving prolonged exposure to special conditions met in confined underground spaces, due to poor ventilation or light, dampness, dust or the noise resulting from the use in such spaces of loud mechanical plant or tools;
(l)   discovery of antiquities and objects of value;
(m)   work above water such as piers;
(n)   work between tides columns to piers;
(o)   work under water such as foundations.

If there are any difficulties due to exceptionally adverse weather conditions the Contractor is only entitled to an extension of time. There is no payment of claims for direct loss and/or expense due to prolongation and disturbance to the regular progress of the contract, unless due to the specified perils of lightning, storm, tempest or flood.

If delay by the Employer causes the period in which the contract was to be executed from a summer-winter-summer contract period to a winter-summer-winter contract period, then the conditions have changed against the Contractor's interest through no fault of his own. The decisions in the cases of *Freeman v Hemsler* (1900) and *Bush v Whitehaven Trustees* (1888) are most important in this regard.

Returning to the possible changed conditions of executing the foundations of a contract, let it be assumed that it is described in the contract documents as a site without having a water table. However, once the excavation is commenced a water table is discovered only 0.40 m below the ground level. The first step for the Contractor is to inform the Architect immediately when the water is discovered and its actual depth below ground level measured and agreed before any more excavation takes place. Only after the Architect agrees the date of discovering the water table and its depth can the Contractor recommence the excavation. At the same time, he can request the raising of star items and star rates due to the changed conditions.

The question of which star items and star rates will arise is best dealt with by reference to the SMM.

SMM6 would invoke clause D.3.1(a) which calls for the ground water table to be decided at the time the various excavations are carried out and to be described as the post water level. Clause D.13.13 (Types of Excavation) would be involved because it requires any excavation below ground water level to be given in cubic metres as extra over all types of excavation, irrespective of depth and also includes for working space as well. Clause D.21 requires earthwork support to excavations below ground water level as defined in clause D.3.1(a) shall be so described and measured from the starting level of the excavation to the full depth. Clause D.22 (Unstable Ground) requires earthwork support to excavations in running silt, running sand and the like to be so described and measured from the starting level of the excavation down to the full depth. The Practice Manual to SMM6 refers to clause D.22 in which the words 'and the like' have been added to the SMM5 wording of 'running silt or running sand' in an attempt to avoid the many arguments that have arisen by limiting the application of the rule literally to 'running silt or running sand', where the same problems pertain with such materials as loose gravel, fly ash, etc. As a guideline, it is suggested that the strata could be said to fall within the intended category only when the newly excavated face will not remain unsupported for a sufficient length of time to allow the necessary support to be inserted.

Clause D.26 of SMM6 (water in the ground) requires an item to be given when excavation is measured below the water level in accordance with clause D.13.13 and item shall be given for keeping the excavations free of ground water.

If the contract documents did not indicate that excavation was in unstable ground but to the contrary, it is now clear that the excavation will also call for star items and star rates, together with excavation described as below the water table.

This additional concept is enshrined in clause D.13.8, although the significance of earthwork supports will be used as counter-argument. However, it can be argued that the extra cost of excavating in unstable ground should be priced in earthwork supports; as long as the extra cost is dealt with adequately, there is no pricing problem. It should not be overlooked that under clause D.40 the treatment of the excavation bottom (level and ram) below ground water level will also attract a star item and star rates.

Should there be a very deep basement excavation, it may be necessary for the Architect to issue a variation instruction for heavy duty interlocking driven sheet piling and measured in accordance with Section E of SMM6.

The requirements of SMM7 are very similar to those of SMM6 concerning the requirement of star items and star rates. The implications of clause 3.7.6 must not be overlooked since the extraction of water from the foundations, drainage trenches and manholes, and external works it may be lumped together in deriving a price.

(c) Significant changes in the quantity of work

Clause 3.7.3 allows for the Contractor to claim star items and star rates for any significant changes in quantity of the work set out in the priced document. Whilst significant changes in quantities must vary considerably in scope, nevertheless it is a principle incorporated into the contract and whether small or large quantities are involved, the Contractor has the right to make a claim. Since in calculations the integration of all dx's leads to x itself, so all the lesser claims eventually lead to a major and substantial claim.

Deciding whether there has been a significant change in a quantity calls for a very rigorous search of the variations and final account. This should be relatively straightforward on a lump sum contract since the comparison between omissions and additions is given by the issue of Architect's instructions for variations. The changes can be researched from the statement of all the final account valuations under clause 3.7 (Valuation of variations) which will be prepared by the Quantity Surveyor, a copy of which will have been sent to the Contractor.

By way of example, let it be assumed that in the drainage section of the contract bill there was a total of 10,000 linear metres of fairly shallow drainage trenches for four diameters of pipe and in the final account there is a total of 15,000 linear metres of deep drainage trenches having many more diameters and generally greater in diameter than in the bill. Such variations must warrant star items and star rates, bearing in mind that with larger diameter pipes a greater depth of excavation is required, and the work content will be significantly increased. This could be further complicated by the discovery of substantial quantities of hard substances needing breaking out, as well as encountering old services which need blanking off.

Clause 3.7.6 might also be invoked with regard to any extra preliminaries.

Should there be a substantial increase in the quantity of surplus excavated material to be removed from the site there could be a claim for a star and a star rate. This would be the case if the Contractor had obtained a source of disposal for a certain quantity of surplus excavated material but the increased quantity could only be partially accommodated. For the balance, the Contractor would have to travel further and pay a higher charge per cubic metre.

A complication to this increased quantity of surplus excavated material could be the discovery of a 1 metre deep layer of contaminated material spread over the area of the excavation as well as the external works. This would require the item to be divided into two parts: one for the disposal of contaminated material to a special location and the other area for the non-contaminated surplus. Special methods of excavation of the contaminated material - to which the Control of Pollution Act 1975 applies - would also need to be taken into account.

In the case of *Kent County Council v Queensborough Rolling Mills* (1990) it was decided that material removed as waste from one site and deposited for a useful purpose at another, albeit that it had been sorted and graded, remained waste in character for the purposes of the Control of Pollution Act 1975: the character of the material is determined at the site of removal not at the site of deposit. It is suggested that when there is a considerable increase to the measured quantity given in the contract bills, the rate cannot be reduced by the Quantity Surveyor because clause 3.7.3 refers to making due allowance to contract rates, which does not imply a reduction in a rate. (Note also clause 4.1.)

Clause 3.7.6 does specifically permit the reduction of any relevant items of a preliminary nature.

Another example is where the contract calls for very expensive hardwood joinery to be fixed in position early on in the contract period and involving 590 units of a particular window. A year later, the Architect issues a variation for one more window. Under clause 3.7.3 a star item and star rate is incurred for the actual cost of the window since it is so far out of sequence. Another example might be where formwork to a soffit was changed to formwork for a cantilevered soffit.

Shortfall
It is possible that there may be a shortfall of a quantity in the contract bills due to an error, ie the item was originally overmeasured (clause 1.4 applies). Should there not be a significant change in the quantity then the omission may be priced under clause 3.7.1 at contract rates. However, if the shortfall involves the Contractor in financial loss he may then seek a due allowance under clause 3.7.3.

For example, assuming the area of formwork to a soffit was 1371 m^2 and is now reduced to 711 m^2 and the rate for the item was £17.70 per m^2.

If this reduction in area causes the number of uses of the formwork to be less, from perhaps six uses down to three uses, then the synthesis of the contract rate and the star item may be as follows:

Estimator's synthesis of the contract rate
Formwork to soffit
The total cost of all materials for the formwork, ie plywood and softwood joists, is taken as £18.00 per m^2.

		£
With 6 uses the cost of formwork	$= \dfrac{£18.00}{6 \text{ uses}}$	= 3.00
Cost of supports		= 1.43
Nails		= 1.05
Carpenter		= 8.57
Labourer		= 1.87
Mould oil		= 0.17
		= 16.09
10% overheads and profit		= 1.61
		= 17.70 m^2

74

Estimator's synthesis of the star rate

	£
With only 3 uses the cost of formwork = $\dfrac{£18.00}{3 \text{ uses}}$	= 6.00
Cost of supports	= 1.43
Nails	= 1.05
Carpenter	= 8.57
Labourer	= 1.87
Mould oil	= 0.17
	= 19.09
10% overheads and profit	= 1.91
	= 21.00 m^2

Dissimilar conditions as well as significant changes in quantity

It is possible under clause 3.7.3 for a variation to require the Contractor to execute work both dissimilar in condition as well as incurring significant change in quantity.

An example of this might be where, under clause 2.6.2, the Architect issues a variation reducing the four entrances to the site to three. It may be that the closing of the fourth entrance may create a far larger haul route. Under another variation the Contractor is required to remove far greater quantities of surplus excavated material from the site and because of this he has to go to another area to deposit the material and perhaps pay a heavier charge for disposal.

Due allowance

Clause 3.7.3 provides that if the conditions under which the Contractor carries out the work shall be different, a 'due allowance' shall be made. The adjective 'due' according to Chambers Twentieth Century Dictionary is 'owed, that ought to be paid or done to another, proper, appointed, under engagement, to be ready, arrive, etc.' It is suggested that this means legally that the Contractor has a right to an additional financial allowance.

As the changes may be of the conditions or differences in the quantity of work, or both, it is necessary to consider the SMM6 definition of a rate or price given in clause 1.4 - Descriptions - which gives full contractual significance of an item in the contract bills and of that which is to be included in the contract rates or prices. The SMM6 clause is as follows:

'A.4 Descriptions

1. *The order of stating dimensions shall be consistent and generally in the sequence of length, width and height. Where that sequence is not appropriate of where ambiguity could arise, the dimensions shall be specifically identified.*

2. *Unless otherwise specifically stated in the bill or herein, the following shall be deemed to be included with all items:*

    (a) *Labour and all costs in connection therewith.*
    (b) *Materials, goods and all costs in connection therewith.*
    (c) *Fitting and fixing materials and goods in position.*
    (d) *Plant and all costs in connection therewith.*
    (e) *Waste of materials.*
    (f) *Square cutting.*
    (g) *Establishment charges, overhead charges and profit.*

3. *Junctions between straight and curved work shall in all cases be included with the work in which they occur.*

4. *Notwithstanding the provisions in this document for labours to be given as linear items, such labours may be given in the description of any linear items of work on which they occur.*

5. *Notwithstanding the provisions in this document for labours to be enumerated, such labours may be given in the description of any enumerated item of work on which they occur.'*

It follows that any three of the following basic elements of the rate or price can be affected by clause 3.7.3 (clause 4.6 of SMM7 is very similar):

  (i) labour and all costs in connection therewith;
  (ii) materials, goods and all costs in connection therewith;
 (iii) plant and all costs in connection therewith.

Each of these elements must, therefore, be rigorously examined to determine what changes have been encountered or incurred. The previous example of a high water table being discovered during the execution of the foundations or an anticipated dry site demonstrates the need to keep very careful cost records. These records should be submitted for checking by the Architect and the clerk of works in order to establish their validity, although it is the Quantity Surveyor who will decide finally whether or not such records are accepted as evidence for the calculation of star rates.

Site photographs are also very important in demonstrating the difficulties in executing work under such different conditions. Alternatively, the best solution may be to seek for daywork payment under clause 3.7.5 but it is essential to obtain the Architect's prior authority and the Quantity Surveyor's approval. (Note also the commentary to clause 3.7.5.) Clause 3.7.4 requires a fair valuation to be made where there is no work of a similar character set out in the priced documents (clause 3.7.1), or to the extent that the valuation does not relate to the execution of additional, or substituted work or the omission of work, or to the extent that the valuation of any work or liabilities directly associated with the instruction cannot reasonably be effected by a valuation by the application of clause 3.7.3. This could be considered to be *Valuation Rule 3.*

Clause 3.7.4 is a difficult clause to interpret, as well as being very wide in its scope regarding valuation. First of all there must be no work of a similar character set out in the priced document. For example, on a contract with substantial areas of brickwork, which now has most of the brickwork omitted and stonework in lieu, would mean there are no contract rates or prices for the stonework in the priced document. In these circumstances a fair valuation will have to be made, since a valuation could not be reasonably effected under clause 3.7.3.

Secondly, the clause speaks of the situation when a valuation does not relate to the execution of additional work. This could arise with variations being made for work of renovation to an existing building where the contract only contained very modest items of adaption. SMM6 requires items executed inside existing buildings to be kept separate (clause A.9.1 of SMM6 or clause 7.1 of SMM7).

Possible directly associated liabilities could be the need to provide air lines for ventilation when the cutting of numerous perforations in existing concrete or brick walls and soffits are producing clouds of dust, as may be the case in an existing basement.

Thirdly, the clause refers to the omission of work for which a valuation would not be reasonably effected by a valuation under clause 3.7.3. From reference to clause 3.7.2 it will be remembered that some omissions could be made using the relevant prices in the priced document: certain amendments could be effected by clause 3.7.8, which deals with the problem of remaining work being executed after the omission of items under clause 3.7.2. However, clause 3.7.4 relates to the actual execution of omissions, which may not be correctly omitted at total contract prices but adjusted to provide for the liabilities which might so arise. Such problems could occur when the omission of an item of contract rates and prices denies the Contractor some payment to which he is fully entitled. For example, the clearing out of formwork prior to concreting using a pneumatic compressor, air lines or hoses, the cost of which is basically included in the rate for provisional items of breaking out hard substances. The Contractor does not locate any such items in the excavations and the provisional items are totally omitted and with them the basic cost of the compressor. An adjustment may then be effected under clause 3.7.4 by a fair valuation of the omitted items. Clause 3.7.6 may apply to the three grounds already given.

'What is meant by a fair valuation?' It can only relate to fair rates and prices, judged by the general tenor of clause 3.7 to 3.7.9. As this is a bilateral contract, 'fair' must relate to both parties. Chambers

Twentieth Century Dictionary defines 'fair' as - impartial, just, equitable, plausible or reasonable but excludes specious, favourable, ponderous, pretty good, passable, fine, out-and-out plausible or pleasing.

Often the adjective 'fair' is used in conjunction with 'and reasonable' but not in clause 3.7.4. Clause 3.7.5 contemplates the need for daywork and may be considered to be **Valuation Rule 4.**

To some extent clause 3.7.5 is correlated to clause 3.7.4, since it states *'Where the appropriate basis of a fair valuation is daywork ...'*. The phrase *'where the appropriate basis ... daywork'* is a matter for the Quantity Surveyor to decide under the contract terms, although subject to negotiation with the Contractor.

Clause 3.7.5 is in two parts, the first part relating to the *'Definition of prime cost of daywork carried out under a building contract'* issued by the RICS and the second to specialised trades and the accepted definition of prime cost agreed between the RICS and BEC. It is noticeable that the normal precautions for rendering details of the labour involved to the Architect each week is not included in clause 3.7.5 but it is strongly recommended that the Contractor in his own interest should do this so as to secure the certainty of payment.

There is much to go wrong with the submission of daywork details and possible errors include:

(a)   failure to use current labour rates;
(b)   failure to use current labour differentials;
(c)   failure to obtain the names and trades of all craftsmen;
(d)   failure to include labourers attending on craftsmen;
(e)   failure to include any materials;
(f)   failure to use current rates for materials;
(g)   failure to include correct quantities of materials;
(h)   failure to include any plant;
(i)   failure to include total hours of plant;
(j)   failure to use correct rates for plant;
(k)   failure to include specialist work;
(l)   failure to use Working Rule Allowances for discomfort, inconvenience and risk;
(m)   failure to charge for converting plant, ie excavator into a crane or vice versa;
(n)   failure to charge for transportation of plant on daywork;
(o)   failure to charge for minimum hire period of a day or week;
(p)   failure to charge for additional equipment such as hoses for a pump or compressor;
(q)   failure to charge correctly for plant specially hired for daywork;
(r)   failure to charge for any hours beyond the four days of 8 and one day of 7 hours or the week of 39 hours.

Contrary to what is generally believed, it is possible to lose out on daywork, bearing in mind the limits of the percentage additions and also the fact that it is often disrupting to the work programme, eg it may incur demolition and rebuilding which puts the contract or works back to status quo and there is no payment for preliminaries.

Clause 3.7.6, referred to in clauses 3.7.2, 3.7.3, 3.7.4 and 3.7.8, states *'the valuation shall include where appropriate any addition to or reduction of any relevant items of a preliminary nature.'*. It may be considered to be **Rule 5 of the Valuation Rules.**

When various items are priced solely in the preliminaries section of the bills on a time-related basis, occasions arise out of variations when they may rank for additional payment. In these circumstances it is possible that there may not be any need for an extension of time because the whole of the works is not involved but only some specific items related to variations issued by the Architect.

Some of the possible items actually priced in the preliminaries section might be:

(a)   scaffolding;
(b)   concrete mixer and batching plant;
(c)   mortar mixers;
(d)   fork lift trucks;
(e)   tower cranes;
(f)   hoists;
(g)   setting out;
(h)   pumping and disposal of surplus water (unless priced in excavation rates);
(i)   transportation, lorries or dumpers;
(j)   small or non-mechanical plant;
(k)   additional supervision by assistant agents or site engineers;
(l)   safety measures.

Examples might be scaffolding being kept standing for six extra weeks because instead of fixing softwood windows as the brickwork progressed, a variation introduced UPVC patent windows instead.

A concrete mixer and batching plant may be delayed by several weeks due to the redesigning sections of the foundations. If variations make it necessary to introduce tower cranes, problems of air trespass could occur. A further example could be where the Contractor is required to supply, temporarily, kentledge for loading and testing pipes and lifts.

On the other hand, if items priced in the preliminaries are not used, then they must be omitted, for example a separate telephone line for the clerk of works.

Clause 3.7.7 makes clear that all financial contractual claims are to be dealt with under clauses 4.11 to 4.12.7.

Also excluded from the valuation of variations is any other direct loss and/or expense for which the Contractor would be reimbursed by payment under any other provision in the conditions, eg the payment of insurance claims under Condition 6.

Clause 3.7.8 has already been touched upon in clauses 3.7.2 and 3.7.4.

It should be recognised in common law that any unanticipated loss, expense or extra cost, for which the Contractor becomes liable during the currency of a contract, apart from variations, has to be paid by the Contractor unless he can find a suitable clause by which he can claim reimbursement.

Clause 3.7.9 is concerned principally with a 'specification and drawings contract' as provided for in the second Recital alternative 'B'. A difficulty which can arise under clause 3.7.9 is the possibility of not having 'the relevant rates and prices' set out to be able to price variations under the valuation rules. In such instances, a fair valuation is to be made. This can be a very complicated procedure with the possibility of it being very disadvantageous to the Contractor.

If SMM7 is to be used then clause 3.7 should be amended to conform with Amendment 4. The additional words at the end of the clause are *'in clauses 3.7.1 to 3.7.9'*. A further paragraph to 3.7 is then added which states, *'All work executed by the Contractor for which an approximate quantity is included in the Contract Documents shall be measured and valued by the Quantity Surveyor in accordance with the rules in clauses 3.7.1 to 3.7.9, for the Valuation of Variations and provisional sum work.'*.

Similarly, clause 3.7.4 has extra words after *'or substituted work'* which run *'or the execution of work for which an approximate quantity is included in the Contract Documents'*.

Similarly, clause 3.7.6 has added *'provided that where the Contract Documents include bills of quantities no such addition or reduction shall be made in respect of compliance with an Architect's instruction for the expenditure of a provisional sum for defined work included in such bills'*.

Similarly, clause 3.7.8 has the addition *'Clause 3.7.8 shall apply to the execution of works for which an approximate quantity is included in the Contract Documents to such extent as the quantity is more or less the quantity ascribed to that work in the Contract Documents and where the Contract Documents include bills of quantities, in compliance with an instruction as to the expenditure of a provisional sum for defined work only to the extent that the instruction for that work differs from the description given for such work in such bills.'*.

Clause 3.8 - Instructions to expend provisional sums

The Architect is required mandatorily to issue instructions as to the expenditure of any provisional sums. Under clause 4.5 all provisional sums in the contract sum must automatically be omitted from the contract sum. (Note the commentary to clause 3.7.)

Clause 3.9 - Levels and setting out

The Architect is required under clause 3.9 to determine any levels which may be required for the execution of the works and shall provide the Contractor, by way of accurately dimensioned drawings, with such information as shall enable him to set out the works.

This clause breaks with tradition in so far as the extent of setting out is usually limited to 'at ground level' but no such limits are place in clause 3.9. On the contrary, the clause not only promises *'accurately dimensioned drawings'* but *'such information as shall enable the Contractor to set out the Works'*, which doubtless the Contractor will use to his fullest advantage. Why the clause should call in this instance for *'accurately' dimensioned drawings'* (because anything other than 'accurate' must be unthinkable) cannot be readily understood, since under clause 1.7 the Architect only has to provide further drawings or details.

The clause also requires the Contractor to be responsible - at no cost to the Employer - for amending any errors arising from his own inaccurate setting out. The significance of inaccurate setting out cannot be overstressed, particularly in the case where the Contractor builds improperly on another person's property.

The last sentence to clause 3.9 allows the Architect, after first obtaining the Employer's consent, to instruct that such errors shall not be amended and an appropriate deduction for such errors not required to be amended shall be made from the contract sum. Presumably, such errors relate to the building in some respects being smaller than the contract drawings and a suitable sum being calculated on that presumption. No statement is given as to that which is to be done if the Contractor's error is to make the building larger than the contract drawings. Will the Employer claim it is not his fault and offer no additional sum for the error?

Apart from the earlier commentary on clauses 3.7 to 3.7.9 the significance must also be recognised of the last paragraph of clause 1.4 in regard to these clauses, which states: *'If any such instructions change the quality or quantity of work deemed to be included in the Contract Sum as referred to in clause 1.2 (Quality or Quantity of Work) or changes any obligations or restrictions imposed by the Employer, the correction shall be valued under clause 3.7 (Valuation of Variations)'.*

Rate agreement safeguard
Until the Contractor is fully prepared to accept a contract or star rate he should not agree but use as a safeguard the term 'provisionally agreeing'.

Clause 3.10 - Clerk of works
It must be stressed that should the Employer appoint a clerk of works, his duty is limited to that as an inspector on behalf of the Employer but under the direction of the Architect. The Contractor should not therefore carry out any directions given by the clerk of works, since he has no jurisdiction to do so.

Clause 3.11 - Work not forming part of the contract
Clause 3.11 contemplates two possibilities concerning *'work not forming part of the Contract'* as follows:
(a)   where the contract documents provide for work (not forming part of the contract) being carried out by the Employer or by persons employed or engaged by the Employer;

(b)   where the contract documents do not so provide.

Where the contract documents provide for work not forming part of the contract, the Contractor is required under clause 3.11 to allow the execution of such work on site of the works concurrent with his execution of the contract works. Provision is made under clauses 2.4.8 and 4.12.3 for any necessary extensions of time and any disturbance to the regular progress of the works involving direct loss and/or expense to be paid for by the financial effect of prolongation and disturbance.

The significance of *'persons employed or engaged by the Employer'* may be that *'persons employed'* are those actually on the staff of the Employer, whilst *'persons engaged'* by the Employer may relate to those persons not on the staff of the Employer. Of course, it may just be a distinction without a difference. Where the contract documents do not provide for work to be carried out not forming part of the contract, the Employer may under the aegis of clause 3.11 seek the consent of the Contractor (which consent shall not be unreasonably withheld) to arrange for the execution of such work.

Contractually, this does not mean that the Employer may seek the omission of the Contractor's own work (whether measured or the subject of provisional sums) and give it to others. Those cases where this was legally established are: *J M Reilly Ltd v Belfast Corporation* (1966)(AC), *Carr v Berriman Property Ltd* (1953), *North West Metropolitan Regional Hospital Board v T A Bickerton Ltd* (1970) and *Commissioner for Main Roads v Reed & Stuart* (1974).

The second paragraph to clause 3.11 states *'every person so employed or engaged shall for the purposes of clauses 6.1 (Injury and damage) and 6.3 (Insurance of the Works) be deemed to be a person for whom the Employer is responsible and not a Sub-contractor.'*.

Clause 3.12 - Instructions as to inspection and tests
Under clause 3.12 the Architect may issue instructions for inspection of any work covered up, or to arrange for or carry out any test of any materials or goods (whether or not already incorporated in the works) or of any executed work.

The question of inspection or testing may have already been included in the contract sum, whether in the specification, schedules of work, or contract bills.

Providing the inspection or test is satisfactory, the Contractor will be reimbursed the cost of opening up, inspecting and testing, together with the cost of making good in consequence thereof and the removal of debris.

Any additional inspection or testing or opening up over and above the contract requirements will also be paid for as instructions, requiring a variation under clause 3.7.

The Contractor will not be paid if any inspection or test shows the materials, goods or work are not in accordance with the contract.

The correlation of the various clauses involved in inspections, testing or opening up of work all in accordance with the contract is shown in Table 3.2.

Table 3.2 Inspection or testing or opening up for work in accordance with the contract

Clause 3.12	Authority for inspections or testing or opening up work
Clause 3.6.1	Provides specifically for the issue of a variation for the removal from the site of any work executed or goods or materials brought on to the site by the Contractor for the purposes of the work (other than work materials or goods which are not in accordance with the contract.).
	NB Works or goods or materials not in accordance with this contract are removed at the Contractor's own expense. (Clause 3.14).
Clause 3.7.5	The opening up, disposal of debris is often the subject of daywork.
Clause 2.4.6	Grounds for an extension of time.
Clause 4.12/2	Direct loss and/or expense because of prolongation and disturbance to the regular progress of the works.

It was decided in the case of *AMF International v Magnet Bowling Ltd and Percy Trentham* (1968) *'that in general an Architect owes no duty to a builder to tell him promptly during the course of construction, even as regards permanent work, when it is going wrong: he may if he wishes leave that to the final stages, notwithstanding that the correction of a fault then may be much more costly to the builder than had his error been pointed out earlier'.*

Clause 3.13 - Instructions following the failure of work, etc.
Clause 3.13.1 requires the Contractor, if a failure of work or of materials and goods is discovered during the carrying out of the works, to state in writing to the Architect the action which he will immediately take, at no cost to the Employer, to establish that there is no similar failure in work already executed or materials or goods already supplied (whether or not incorporated in the works).

This could arise if a reinforced concrete suspended slab had collapsed and the Employer was concerned about the stability of any other suspended slab. A more difficult problem would be if there were 70 piles and after testing four of the piles failed a loading test. What is to happen then? It would be unreasonable to expect the Contractor to test load the remaining 66 piles at his own cost. Some degree of compromise will obviously have to be considered and perhaps wide ranging guarantees also.

Both clauses 3.31.1 and 3.13.2 set out the elaborate contractual procedures to be followed, together with specific time periods, when disagreements arise from the Contractor's refusal to comply with Architect's instructions, concluding with arbitration under clauses 9 and 9.6 (whether or not that clause is stated in the Appendix to apply). Immediate arbitration is often very necessary in these circumstances.

The Contractor will have to be very sure of his ground when he challenges the Architect's instructions. He will have to also obtain very experienced professional assistance, including legal advice, as with certain issues the result of failing to comply with the Architect's instructions could be financially significant and very time-consuming.

It is interesting that in the case of *Warwick University v Cementation Chemicals* (1989)(CA) the two Appeal Judges decided that it had not been shown that Cementation Chemicals Ltd knew or should have known that damage was likely to occur from the resin injection. The epoxy resin adhesive was originally injected behind a tiled facade which caused the tiling to crack. This perhaps gives an inkling over the reasoning or the attitude to these difficulties by a court!

Practice Note PH/1/84 seeks to suggest a possible solution on page 5 stating *'depending on the failure and the circumstances, progressive sampling or other methods may be considered sufficient, without opening up or testing every similar item of work'*. This is only a suggestion and not necessarily a contractual fact.

Clause 3.14 - Instructions as to removal of work
The Architect is given authority to issue an instruction for a variation to *'remove from the site any work executed or materials or goods brought thereon by the Contractor for the purpose of the Works other than work or materials or goods not in accordance with the Contract'*. Under clause 3.6.1, however, the requisite instructions in regard to the removal from the site of any work, materials or goods which are not in accordance with this contract are given under clause 3.14.

The Contractor only has to remove those items from the site which the Architect explicitly states in the instruction. Unless the Architect issues such instructions there is no contractual grounds for the Contractor to remove the items. Even so, there must be limits to the Architect's instructions since it is suggested that legally and practically it is impossible to require the Contractor to remove a coat of paint from the site!

Clause 3.15 - Instruction as to postponement
The fact that the Architect may issue instructions in regard to the postponement of any work to be executed under the provisions of the contract is provided for in clause 3.15.

It should be realised that the Architect cannot postpone the works themselves only 'any work' because it is held that 'any' is not the equivalent of 'all'. It would be another matter if the clause stated 'all or any part thereof'. Chambers Twentieth Century Dictionary defines 'part' as 'something less than the whole'.

The postponement of the works themselves could be construed as rescission by the Employer. It is also important to realise that clause 2.2 defers the giving of possession by the Employer, it is not a postponement under clause 3.15.

The principle of postponement under IFC84 is a very powerful weapon in the hands of the Contractor, since the contractual length of postponement is limited to the determination period for the Contractor, ie a continuous period of one month for various grounds set out in clauses 7.5.3(a) to 7.5.3(d). A month is taken to be a calendar month since the lunar month of 28 days is not specifically mentioned. It has to be a continuous period of one month, the actual time being from midnight of the 1st of the month until midnight of the last day of the month.

If the postponement is one day short of a month it is not a continuous period of a month. It is possible for an Architect to postpone one section of the site for, say, 26 days and then release the postponement of that particular section of the site and then impose a postponement for, say, 26 days on another section of the site and so on. A continuous period of one month is essentially a very short period and in the circumstances of a major fire, the Architect, rather than issue a postponement, should elect instead to grant extensions of time.

An exception to a postponement of a continuous period of one month involving determination is when the loss or damage to the works is occasioned by one or more of the specified perils caused by the negligence of the Contractor, his servants or agents or by any Sub-contractor, his servants or agents. This is specifically set out in clause 7.8.2. The grounds by which a postponement may allow the Contractor to determine his own employment are given in clauses 6.3, 5.4.3, 7.5.1 to 7.5.3(d) and 7.8.1, 7.8.2 and 7.9.

The Contractor must also follow the contract requirement concerning determination given in clause 7.5. (Note the commentary to clause 7.5.)

CONDITION 4 - PAYMENT

Clause 4.1 - Contract sum
Clause 4.1 is very important and clearly establishes that IFC84 is a lump sum contract. It states that the contract sum shall not be adjusted or altered in any way otherwise than in accordance with the express provisions of the Conditions. The calculation of the final certificate commences with the value of the lump sum contract from which is added or deducted sums of money as given in the express conditions of the contract such as contingencies, variations, daywork, contractual claims, price fluctuations, insurance claims, insurance premiums under clause 2.1 (fourth paragraph), inspection or testing fees, omission of provisional sums, provisional quantities, any additions thereof, any omissions under clauses 3.9 and 4.9, as well as any additions under clause 3.13.2 and corrections of errors under clause 1.4.

The second half of clause 4.1 is also very important and states, subject to clause 1.4, a saving clause concerning Architect's instructions as to inconsistencies, errors or omissions by the Architect, Quantity Surveyor or other agents of the Employer. The Contractor is responsible for any error or omission, whether of arithmetic or not, in the compilation of the contract sum which shall be deemed to have been accepted by the parties.

This means that the rates and prices in the contract priced document are binding to both parties. Neither can the Quantity Surveyor price the quantity in the bills at a wrong rate and then adjust the rate for any quantity exceeding the quantity in the contract bills. That a wrong rate applies equally to any increased quantity was decided on the judgment in the case of *Dudley Corporation v Parsons & Morris* (1959)(CA).

Where clause 4.1 states *'Any error of omission, whether of arithmetic or not'*, it means that if the Contractor makes an error in the selection of a proper labour constant, in quantity of materials or value of plant he has to stand by his rate or price. The Contractor may also be in error by failing to price specifically an item in the bills. The common law in regard to this issue is found in the case of *M V Gleeson Ltd v Sleaford* (1953) where the Contractor failed to price a substantial portion of a bills of quantities. There were rates elsewhere in the bills of quantities but the Judge held that there was no error in the bills of quantities, only in the Contractor's pricing of them and he could recover nothing. Clause 4.1 is legally binding in regard to all the Contractor's pricing errors. Those unilateral errors which were undiscovered by either party before entering into the contract were dealt with in the judgment of the case of *Riverplate Properties v Paul* (1974)(CA) and cannot be corrected after entering into the contract. Problems can arise should errors be discovered before entering into a contract which cause the lowest tenderer's contract sum to become greater than the second lowest tenderer's estimate. The Contractor would have to reconsider his position in such circumstances and may possibly have to forego any correction of his contract sum. This is a commercial judgment which can only be made by the Contractor.

Clause 4.2 - Interim payments
The intention of the contract is to have monthly financial certificates as evidenced by the Appendix. Under clause 4.2 it is also possible to have a period of one month between interim certificates, unless otherwise decided by stating in the blank space provided on the Appendix. The reference in the Appendix is to *'Period of interim certificates if interval is not one month'*. One month is a very suitable period and is the one normally used. Clause 4.2 itself restates these facts but goes on to state that the date of the first certificate is to be calculated one month from the date of possession stated in the Appendix. It is mandatory for the Architect to certify the amount of interim certificates. The Employer has to pay the value of interim certificates within 14 days of the date of the certificate. It is not the date of receipt of the interim certificate by the Employer but the date of the interim certificate which governs the interpretation of 'within fourteen days'.

The reason for the second paragraph to clause 4.2 is a little obscure since it states, *'Interim valuations shall be made by the Quantity Surveyor wherever the Architect considers them to be necessary for the purpose of ascertaining the amount to be stated as due in an interim payment'*. Whereas the third paragraph states *'that the amount of the interim certificate shall be the total amounts in clauses 4.2.1 and 4.2.2 at a date not more than 7 days before the date of the certificate, less any sums previously certified for payment'*. Surely the third paragraph almost entirely over-rides the second paragraph?

Clause 4.2.1 - Retention

The third paragraph to clause 4.2 in the second sentence states *'These amounts are:'*.

Clauses 4.2.1(a), (b) and (c) give details of the amounts to be included in the interim certificates, all of which are subject to a 5% retention.

The amount to be certified under clause 4.2.1(a) is the total value of work properly executed by the Contractor, (less 5% retention), including any items valued in accordance with clause 3.7 (valuation of variations), together with, where applicable, any adjustment of the value under clause 4.9(b) (formulae adjustment) but excluding any restoration, replacement or repair of loss or damage or removal and disposal of debris, which in clauses 6.3B.3.5 and 6.3C.4.4 are treated as if they were a variation.

The interim certificate can only include for work properly executed by the Contractor. To include any improperly executed work would be a breach of contract. Where improperly executed work is included in error it must be deducted from the next interim certificate. If the Contractor were to go into liquidation between interim certificates and the first included for some temporarily executed work, then the Architect becomes liable to repay to the Employer the cost of such work. This was decided in the House of Lords case of *Sutcliffe v Thackrah* (1974).

Clause 4.2.1(b) permits the total value of the materials and goods to be included in an interim certificate (less 5% retention), providing they have been reasonably and properly and not prematurely delivered to or adjacent to the works for incorporation therein and which are adequately protected against weather and other casualties. (Note the commentary to clause 1.10.)

'Casualties' according to Chambers Twentieth Century Dictionary means amongst other things: accidents; misfortunes; losses; mishaps; disasters and negligence, for which the Contractor is legally and financially liable simpliciter unless proven to the contrary.

Clause 4.2.1(c) permits, at the discretion of the Architect, for the value of any off-site goods and materials (less 5% retention) to be included in an interim certificate. It might have been thought necessary for the protection of the Employer's property, for clear safeguards also to be given in clause 4.2.1(c), but doubtless they may be given elsewhere in the contract documents.

Clause 4.2.2 allows for a 100% inclusion of a number of amounts related to contractual claims, which may be included in an interim certificate. These are:

(a) Clause 2.1   In paragraph 3 of clause 2.1 provision is made for an additional insurance premium for a deferred start to the contract.
(b) Clause 3.12   Inspection or tests which are in accordance with the contract.
(c) Clause 4.9(a)   Supplemental Condition C - tax etc and fluctuations.
(d) Clause 4.10   Fluctuations - named persons.
(e) Clause 4.11   Claims for prolongation and disturbance.
(f) Clause 5.1   Statutory obligations.

(g)	Clause 6.2.4	Insurance liability by the Employer - if clause 6.2.4 of the Appendix is operated.
(h)	Clause 6.3A.4	Insurance claims and use of monies (insurance by the Contractor).
(i)	Clause 6.3B.2	Failure of the Employer to insure - Contractor may pay premiums instead.
(j)	Clause 6.3B.3.5	Insurance claims and use of monies (insurance by the Employer).
(k)	Clause 6.3C.3	Failure by the Employer to insure - Contractor may pay premiums instead.
(l)	Clause 6.3C.4.4	Insurance claims and use of monies. (insurance by the Employer).

The total inclusion of such amounts are to the extent that they have been ascertained and also that deductions have been made under clause 3.9 (levels and setting out) due to culpability by the Contractor. There can be another deduction made under clause 4.2.2 by reason of clause 4.9(a). Clause 4.9(a) states the contract sum, less any amount included therein for any work to be executed by a named person as a Sub-contractor under clause 3.3, shall be adjusted in accordance with Supplemental Condition C - which deals with contribution, levy and tax fluctuations.

Supplemental Conditions are found in a separate booklet published by RIBA Publications Ltd. They are usually referred to as 'limited fluctuations'.

The purpose of the deduction of named persons from the contract sum is to allow the interim certificate calculations to be based on that reduced value in order to calculate the value of price fluctuations for any change in contribution, levy or tax fluctuations, which may be a deduction as well as possible addition to the contract sum and which is not subject to a 5% retention. The cross-reference of clause 4.9(a) to clause 3.3 possibly relates to clauses 3.3.1 or more likely to 3.3.2(a) which is the inclusion of a provisional sum under clause 3.8 which allows the Architect to have work executed by a named person who is to be employed by the Contractor as Sub-contractor. (See also clause 3.8.)

Clause 4.2.2 does not require any deduction for clause 4.9(b) and it will be recalled that any payment due under clause 4.9(b) is paid under clause 4.2.1 and is subject to a 5% retention.

There may also be a deduction under clause 4.10 for named persons for any sum which would have been excluded under clause 33.4.7 or 34.7.1 of the Sub-Contract Conditions NAM/SC, as well as any deduction by reason of price fluctuation.

Clause 4.3 - Interim payment on practical completion
When practical completion is reached and certified by the Architect under clause 2.9, the Contractor is entitled to a reduction in the retention from 5 to 2.5% as far as clause 4.2.1(a) is concerned and an interim (penultimate) certificate by the Architect is to be made within 14 days. There is no retention to be deducted from the items listed in clause 4.2.2.

Clause 4.4 - Interest in percentage retained
Clause 4.4 deals with the situation where the Employer is not a local authority. When retention is deducted in interim or penultimate certificates the Employer's (legal) interest in the retention fund is fiduciary as trustee for the Contractor. This involves the law of trusts, which means that

the retention fund always remains the Contractor's but is held in trust until the time of its ultimate release under the final certificate (clauses 4.6 and 4.7). The Contractor must ensure that the retention fund is placed in a separate bank account of the Employer and properly described as a retention fund for the actual building contract concerned. If this is not specifically accomplished and the Employer goes into liquidation, the liquidator will argue that since there is no special arrangement for separating the retention fund he alone is entitled to the money and not the Contractor.

This is not an issue which can be put off by some vague promises from the Employer but must be insisted upon by the Contractor to the letter of the law. If not, he must be prepared to suffer the financial consequences.

The Employer is not required to invest the retention fund nor place it on deposit with any benefit to the Contractor.

The Employer may retain all or part of the whole retention fund only if he has a claim for any amount to which he is entitled under the contract and is contractually permitted to deduct any sum due or become due to the Contractor. Liquidated damages for non-completion under clause 2.7 would be a contractual provision for which the Employer could retain part or all of the retention fund. Clause 2.10 is another such clause. (Also note clause 4.6.)

Clause 4.5 - Computation of adjusted contract sum

The heading to clause 4.5, '*Computation of adjusted Contract Sum*' is normally known as the final account but it is a term never employed by the JCT. It is used freely in other standard forms of contract, such as the ICE Conditions, 5th Edition and the GC/Works/1-Editions 2 and 3.

A timetable is set out in clause 4.5 which requires the Contractor to provide the Quantity Surveyor with all documents reasonably required for the purposes of the adjustment of the contract sum. Not later than three months after receipt by the Architect or Quantity Surveyor, as the case may be, of the aforesaid documents, a statement of all the final valuations under clause 3.7 (valuation of variations) shall be prepared by the Quantity Surveyor and a copy of the computation of the adjusted contract sum sent to the Contractor.

The second paragraph to clause 4.5 states that the adjustment of the contract sum shall be in accordance with clause 3.7, valuation of variations and provisional sum work, together with any price formula fluctuation adjustment under clause 4.9(b) and with the amounts together with any deductions, referred to in clause 4.2.2, as finally ascertained, less all provisional sums and any amount to be deducted under clause 2.10.

In the event of SMM7 being used it is necessary, under Amendment No. 4, to amend clause 4.5 by adding after 'provisional sums' and before 'and any amount, etc.' the following statement: '*and the value of any work for which an Approximate Quantity is included in the Contract Document.*'

Clause 4.6 - Issue of final certificate

It is vitally important for the Contractor to know exactly what is the legal significance of a final certificate and clause 4.6 does this quite successfully. The two fundamental issues are that the work has been satisfactorily carried out and completed in conformity with the demands of the contract and that a statement as to the total financial amount of the contract has also been given. There is an exclusion as to the finality of the final certificate if there should be any matter which is the subject of proceedings commenced before or within 28 days after the date of the final certificate. This means that when the Contractor recieves his copy of the final certificate he has a maximum of 28 days in which to lodge a Notice of Arbitration (Article 5 and Condition 9) or legal proceedings under clause 4.11, which refers to *'any other rights or remedies which the Contractor may possess.'*

If the Contractor has already been given Notice of Arbitration or legal proceedings before the issue of the final certificate, this will prevent the certificate being final.

An example of a Contractor failing to give notice within the stated contract period (14 days), which cost his legal right to go to arbitration or litigation, is the case of *Emson Contractors Ltd v Protea Estates Ltd* (1987). The issue of a final certificate provides evidence that the quality of materials and the standard of workmanship is, where the provisions of clause 1.1 apply, to the reasonable satisfaction of the Architect. Presumably, the quality of any materials or standard of workmanship not subject to the proviso of clause 1.1 must be in conformity with the conditions of contract.

Another exclusion to the finality of the final certificate, *'save in regard to any accidental inclusion or exclusion of any item or any arithmetical error in any computation'*, is set out in clause 4.7.

The final certificate must ensure that *'any necessary effect has been given to all the terms of this Contract that require additions or adjustments or deductions from the Contract Sum'*.

It is also necessary *'that all and only such extensions of time, if any, are as due under clause 2.3, have been given'* are properly dealt with in the final certificate.

The final paragraph to clause 4.7 is unique in the JCT standard forms in that it is very explicit. It states *'that the reimbursement of direct loss and/or expense, if any, to the Contractor pursuant to clause 4.11 is in final settlement of all and any claims which the Contractor has or may have arising out of the occurrence of any of the matters referred to in clause 4.12 whether such claim be for breach of contract, duty of care, statutory duty or otherwise'*.

Clause 4.7

This clause is most useful in drawing the threads of the final account and claims together in clear and concise language.

The last paragraph of clause 4.11, which states that *'the provisions of clause 4.11 are without prejudice to any other rights or remedies which the Contractor may possess'*, means that the reference in clause 4.7 as to the final settlement of all claims ... *'whether such claim be for breach of contract, duty of care, statutory duty or otherwise'* must be strictly limited to those claims which arise from contractual claim clauses. Those claims which do not arise from contractual claim clauses are the subject of clause 4.11 and are not to be settled by the Architect and Quantity Surveyor. They are the subject of either arbitration or litigation.

Clause 4.8 - Effect of certificates other than final

Clause 4.8 makes it absolutely clear that apart from clause 4.7, no certificate of the Architect shall of itself be conclusive evidence that any work, materials or goods to which it relates are in accordance with this contract. This is the common law situation and allows the correction of a previous certificate in an ensuing certificate should faulty work have been erroneously included. Once an interim certificate has been issued by the Architect to the Employer it cannot be corrected, if in error, until the next interim certificate. (Note the following commentary specifically in this regard.)

The common law of certificates - generally

It will be remembered that a certificate is a written statement by a person who has authority under a contract which involves his judgment concerning some issue or another within his authority provided by the clauses of the contract. If a pro forma certificate is not used it is imperative for the Architect in his letter to state that it is a certificate, otherwise it will be void. (See the decision in *Token Construction v Charlton Estates* (1973) where a certificate was defined as *'The expression in a definite form of the exercise of the opinion of the Architect in relation to some matter provided for by the terms of the Contract'*. See also *Minster Trust Ltd v Trap Tractors Ltd* (1954.)

A case which clearly sets forth the common law of interim certificate is that of *Dunlop & Ranken Ltd v Hendall Steel Structures Ltd (Pitchers Ltd Garnishees)* (1957)(CA) which, although dealing with the problem of a Sub-contractor, is equally applicable to a Main Contractor. It was held in this case that until the Architect's certificate had been given there was no debt due. It will be recalled that in clause 4.6 the final amount to be certified under a final certificate would *'be a debt payable as the case may be by the Employer to the Contractor or by the Contractor to the Employer, subject to any amounts properly deductible by the Employer'*. It uses the term 'due payable' (or if legally preferred 'debt due') as being the correct terminology for a due 'payment'. This decision makes it clear that payment under the contract can only be made by virtue of an interim, penultimate or final certificate by the Architect. Failure by the Employer to make a payment after receiving the Architect's certificate within the period stated on the certificate can lead to the Contractor determining his own employment under clauses 7.5.1 and 7.5.2, providing the provisions of clause 7.5 are strictly followed. The Architect would be committing a breach of contract if he wilfully refused to issue a certificate when one is contractually due under clauses 4.2, 4.3 and 4.6.

In the case of *London Borough of Camden v Thomas MacInnery & Sons* (1986) the Judge stated *'This means that each time an interim certificate is issued the Architect is only expressing a provisional view that the Works have been properly executed up until the date when he makes his certificate'*. He is plainly free to take a fresh view each time he issues an interim certificate and his opinion about the quality of work cannot become conclusive - until he issues his final certificate.

In the case of *Lubenham Fidelities & Investment Co Ltd v South Pembrokeshire District Council &*

Another (1985)(CA) it was decided that *'where in a building contract it was agreed that the Employer's Architect should issue interim certificates stating the amount due to the Contractor from the Employer and that the Contractor would be entitled to payment therefor within a specified period, the Employer was bound to pay the amount stated in the Certificate even though the amount was wrong and the certificate contained patent and latent errors.'* The value attributed to the constituent parts by the Architect in his certificate could never be more than approximate: it depended upon his expert opinion as the person to whom the parties had entrusted that function. Any error could be remedied by adjustments in subsequent certificates.'. The use of the phrase *'patent or latent errors'* possibly means 'obvious' or 'concealed' errors.

One of the patent errors was the deduction of liquidated damages by the Architect from an interim certificate, instead of certifying the full amount and then for the Employer to deduct the value of the liquidated damages himself!

Interim certificates can only be issued at the periods given in the contract or its Appendix. The not infrequent practice of having additional interim certificates between monthly certificates is not correct. It was decided in the case of *Hickman v Roberts* (1915) that an Architect in his certificates must not be influenced by the Employer. (In view of the various points of law that keep arising there is kept in the Courts a reference work called the 'White Book', and it should be known that where there is general accord on a legal point it is registered in the 'White Book' for further reference.

Clause 4.9 - Fluctuations

Any price fluctuations which arise on a contract are the subject of choice under clause 4.9 for the Main Contractor and decided by invoking either clause 4.9(a) or clause 4.9(b) in the Appendix.

Clause 4.9(a) is concerned with Supplementary Conditions C1-7 inclusive. If any percentage addition is to be made on the contribution, levy and tax fluctuations, it must be given in the appropriate place on the Appendix against clause 4.9(a) and C7. This percentage is normally not more than 10%.

The footnote (o) to clause 4.9(a) in the Appendix states that in accordance with clause 4.9 of Supplemental Condition D is not stated to apply, then Supplemental Condition C applies. This means there must be one price fluctuation clause to be operated under the contract. (Note that clause 4.9(a) ends with the statement *'unless'*.)

Clause 4.9(b) is concerned with Supplemental Condition D - formula fluctuation is stated in the Appendix to apply and contract bills are included in the contract documents.

It is necessary to implement the instructions to the Appendix concerning clause 4.9(b), which first of all states *'Supplemental conditions either 'applies' or 'does not'*. Secondly-Clause D1-formula rules needs the date of rule 3: Base Date to be inserted on the Appendix. Also, rule 3 needs a percentage to be stated on the Appendix (but not to exceed 10%) in regard to the non-adjustment element. Further, a decision has to be make on the Appendix whether Part I or Part II of rules 10 and

30(i) is to apply. Price fluctuations clauses can be an addition to or a deduction from the contract sum. This was the case of contribution, levy and tax levy a few years ago, when it did involve several reductions of contributions and the inevitable need to make deductions from the contract sum. It will be recalled that under clause 4.2.2, specific reference is made inregard to deduction under clause 4.9(b). Clause 4.9 requires the deduction of the value of work to be executed by a named person as a Sub-contractor from the contract sum under clause 3.3.

The financial reason for this adjustment lies in the fact that the price fluctuation causes for the Main Contractor and for the named person as a Sub-contractor may differ.

Clause 4.10 - Fluctuations: Named persons

Clause 4.10 is linked to the previous clause and states *'in respect to any amount included in the Contract Sum for work to be executed by a named person as mentioned in clause 4.9 - the Contract Sum shall be adjusted by the net amount which is payable to or allowable by the named person under clauses 33 and 34 (as applicable) of the Sub-Contract Conditions NAM/SC.'.*

Clause 33 deals with the contribution, levy and tax fluctuations whilst clause 34 deals with formula adjustment fluctuations.

There is a correlation between clause 4.10 and clause 4.2.2 since there may be deductions under clause 4.10 for any reduction brought about by price fluctuations. (See commentary to clause 4.9.)

Clause 4.11 - Disturbance of regular progress

Clause 4.11 deals with prolongation and disturbance to the regular progress of the work where the Contractor has been granted extensions of time for which the Employer is financially liable. Claims not covered by contractual claim clauses are the subject of arbitration or litigation according to the last paragraph of clause 4.11.

It is stated in clause 4.11 *'if, upon written application being made to him by the Contractor, within a reasonable time of it becoming apparent, the Architect is of the opinion that the Contractor has incurred or is likely to incur direct loss and/or expense, for which he would not be reimbursed by a payment under any other provision of this Contract ...'.*

It will have been observed in clause 2.3 that the conjunction 'if' is used twice. Whenever there is a claim it obviously needs exploring by both parties involved at the actual time it occurs in order that the facts may be readily obtained and decisions made. This is the reason for the phrase in clause 4.11 *'within a reasonable time of it becoming apparent ...'.*

The examination of a specific claim at the time of its occurrence is not always understood to be vitally imperative for both parties.

A strict limit is imposed on contractual claims, clause 4.11 making it plain that the Contractor must not have been paid under any other provision of the contract. This may occur by the recovery of additional valuation under clauses 3.7 to 3.7.9 overlapping at the time of the disturbance or in regard to clause 3.7.6 payment or the contiguous effect of daywork or price fluctuations.

It must be borne in mind that clause 3.7.7 strictly forbids any allowances to be made in valuation under clauses 3.7 to 3.7.9 *'for any effect upon the regular progress of the Works or for any other direct loss and/or expense for which the Contractor would be reimbursed by payment under any provision in the Conditions.'*. Payment excluded from clause 3.7.7 is payable instead under clause 4.11.

Clause 4.11 is divided into two separate aspects of the contract viz.

(i) Clause 4.11(a) The deferment of the Employer giving possession of the site under clause 2.2, where that clause is stated to be applicable.
(ii) Clause 4.11(b) The regular progress of the works or part of the works being materially affected by any one or more matters referred to in clause 4.12.

Clause 4.11(a)
The direct loss and/or expense under clause 4.11(a) relates to the cause of deferment and must involve some of the following matters:

(i) effect of marshalling resources for initial delivery to the site;
(ii) cost of storing all temporary offices, toilet facilities, storage sheds and accommodation for clerk of works off-site ready for delivery to site when possession is eventually made available;
(iii) hire cost of items in (ii);
(iv) cost of storing all essential plant;
(v) hire cost of all items in (iii);
(vi) costs of site agent, foreman, site engineer, key staff and other essential staff, staff on standby;
(vii) cost of site Quantity Surveyor on standby;
(viii) any head office direct loss and/or expense incurred by deferment.

The contractor will be expected to mitigate financially as much of the cost of these items as is possible under the circumstances, ie by at least part-time seconding staff to other sites.

Clause 4.11(b)
The direct loss and/or expense under clause 4.11(b) relates to the regular progress of the works or part of the works being materially affected by one or more of the matters referred to in clause 4.12.

All the matters referred to in clause 4.12 carry a financial liability for the Employer.

It must be realised that any extension of time granted under clause 2.2 must mean the entire works have been delayed (or are likely to be delayed), whereas under clause 4.11(b), by contrast, the direct loss and/or expense can relate to either: the regular progress of the works or part of the works being materially affected by any one or more of the matters referred to in clause 4.12. This distinction between clause 2.3 and clause 4.11(b) is not always appreciated by some Contractors and it can seriously mislead them into believing that the two clauses are identical in scope when in fact they are not.

It is evident that all matters listed in clauses 4.12 to 4.12.7 may provide for prolongation direct loss and/or expense, provided extensions of time have been granted under clause 2.3.

By contrast, the disturbance to the regular progress of the works or part thereof does not need the granting of any extensions of time per se. Further, even although the work has slowed down but not sufficient to warrant an extension of time, the Contractor may have incurred direct loss and/or expense due to the Employer or the Architect's default.

Disturbance to the regular progress of the works or part thereof must involve disruption, dislocation, loss of efficiency and uneconomic working.

In the event of a claim (clause 4.7) being made under clause 4.11 the Architect shall ascertain, or shall instruct the Quantity Surveyor to ascertain, such loss and expense incurred. Whilst in the case of *Burden v Swansea Corporation* (1957) it was decided the Architect was not bound to accept the Quantity Surveyor's opinions or valuation, it would appear certain under clause 4.11 that if the Architect specifically and mandatorily instructs the Quantity Surveyor to ascertain, then the Architect in such circumstances would be bound by his ascertainment.

It will be observed that whilst *'direct loss and/or expense'* is given in clause 4.11 (paragraph one), 4.11(b) refers to *'such loss and expense'* incurred. This possibly is a distinction without a difference but, nevertheless, the clause may well be litigated in regard to this difference in terminology on some future occasion.

There is a restriction to clause 4.11(b) in that it states *'the amount ascertained is dependant upon the Contractor in support of his application shall submit such information required by the Architect or the Quantity Surveyor as is reasonably necessary for the purposes of this clause.'*.

The initial conjunction and noun 'if' demonstrates that claims are not a foregone conclusion and that there may be considerable doubt about their authenticity. Contractual claims must, therefore, be founded on appropriate contractual clauses and completely backed with proven facts and evidence.

The verb transitive 'ascertainment' given in clause 4.11 means to find out with certainty. In English the prefix 'as' added to a word such as 'certain' intensifies the degree of certainty; in other words to be as accurate as it is possible to be. Therefore, this must be the approach of either the Architect or the Quantity Surveyor as the case may be.

There is a school of thought which believes that the ascertainment must be by the Architect or Quantity Surveyor alone, without any submitted claim being made by the Contractor. This is erroneous and can be easily frustrated by the Architect refusing to consider any claim until the Contractor submits full details. If the Contractor still refuses to submit details and the Architect is also obdurate, the Contractor will have to then either resort to arbitration or litigation, both of which logistically can be very long and unrewarding and where the Contractor will have to submit the fullest claim details to the arbitrator or the judge.

Why not provide the details at the first opportunity and avoid long delays and possible eventual defeat over producing the details of the claims?

It must be realised that the Contractor must always submit a claim, since a threat to submit a claim is not a submitted claim. Whilst a civil engineering contract, the decision in the case of *Humber Oils Terminal Trusts Ltd v Hersent Off Shores Ltd* (1981)(BLR-16) is nevertheless very interesting in regard to the failure to actually submit a claim!

Clause 4.11(b) speaks of the regular progress of the works or part of the works being materially affected. The adverb 'materially' according to Chambers Twentieth Century Dictionary means amongst other things 'in a considerable or important degree'.

Therefore, this stresses that the term *'materially affect'* in clause 4.11(b) is not a trivial matter but sufficiently important to disturb the regular progress of the works or part thereof. A material fact in the case of *Saker v Secretary of State for Social Services* (1988)(CA) was defined as one which might influence the judgment of a court. This indicates the quality or strength of a fact. Rule 7(1) of Litigation Order 18 requires every pleading to state material facts only. The material facts will have to be proven by evidence. Evidence may consist of relevant evidence, oral evidence, admissible evidence, documentary evidence, direct evidence, circumstantial evidence and real evidence. The Contractor must be aware of coincidences because they may raise the gravest doubt or suspicion. To employ a coincidence it is necessary to rely solely on the 'unreliable'.

If in clause 2.1 the Contractor is mandatorily required *'to begin and regularly diligently proceed with the Works and shall complete the same on or before the date stated in the Appendix'*, then if the Employer or the Architect disturbs that regular progress of the works or part thereof, it is only reasonable that the Contractor should be reimbursed for the direct loss and/or expense incurred.

The common law of mitigation equally applies, although not expressly stated under clause 4.11(b) as it did in clause 2.3.

The legal doctrine of mitigation is found in the case of *British Westinghouse Electric & Manufacturing Co Ltd v Underground Electric Rail Co of London* (1912)(HOL).

Clause 4.12 - Matters referred to in clause 4.11
The matters which may have caused disturbance to the works or part thereof are listed in clause 4.12.

However, before dealing with the various matters (grounds) listed in clause 4.12, it should be noted that clauses 2.3 and 4.11 employ the use of the conjunction 'if' and the likelihood of the Contractor succeeding with his contractual claims lies in his ability to change the doubt into certainty.

The first step must be to make a written application to the Architect stating that he has incurred or is likely to incur direct loss and/or expense. In normal circumstances, the Contractor should always notify the Architect at the earliest moment of his intention to make and register a contractual claim.

However, it is possible for a claim to be 'out of time', whether due to the Statute of Limitations or to the legal doctrine of laches. By being punctual with the submission of contractual claims, the hurdle of 'being out of time' does not arise.

In the phrase *'direct loss and/or expense'* the adjective 'direct' has a limiting effect on the use of the word and does not consequently extend to 'indirect' loss because it is probably too remote. For a legal definition of 'direct' attention is drawn to the case of *Saint Line v Richardson Westgate Ltd* (1940).

In the case of *F G Minter & Drake & Scull v Welsh Hospital Technical Services Organisation* (1980) it was decided that the adjective 'direct' must exclude the second rule of the two rules given in *Hadley v Baxendale* (1854).

The financial loss involved in a contractual claim may arise from the fact that a Contractor expects to be paid for something under the contract but because of certain events and omissions finds that he will not be paid. He therefore seeks redress by having the 'loss' reimbursed.

In regard to 'expense' it is suggested that events occur which now cause the Contractor to incur unforeseen expense and for which he seeks reimbursement. It is the singular transitive verb 'expense' which is used and is not the plural equivalent of 'expenses'.

The legal doctrine enshrined in clause 4.11 is restituto in integrum, ie the restoration to the original financial position to which the Contractor is entitled to be placed as far as finance is concerned. The contractual phrase 'direct loss and/or expense' is the spelling out of the legal term 'damages'. The fundamental basis of contract law concerning a breach of contract is based on the case of *Hadley v Baxendale* (1854). It has already been previously stated that of the two rules given in that case the adjective 'direct' excludes the second rule.

The first rule of *Hadley v Baxendale* is stated by the Judges as, *'We think the proper rule in such a case as the present is this: where two parties have made a contract which one of them has broken, the damages which the other party ought to receive in respect of such a breach of contract should be, either such as may fairly and reasonably considered arising naturally, ie according to the usual course of things, from such breach of contract itself.'*

Clause 4.12 lists all the contractually acceptable matters (grounds) for contractual claims of disturbance to the regular progress of the works or part thereof as follows:
Clause 4.12.1 Late instructions;
Clause 4.12.2. Work opened up and goods or materials found to be in accordance with contract under clause 3.12;

Clause 4.12.3 Execution of work not forming part of the contract by others under clause 3.11;

Clause 4.12.4 Failure by the Employer to supply materials and/or goods;

Clause 4.12.5 Postponement under clause 3.15;

Clause 4.12.6 Failure by the Employer to give ingress or egress to the site of the works;

Clause 4.12.7 Architect's instructions under clauses 1.4, 3.6, 3.8 and named persons under clause 3.3.

The seven grounds given above permit the Contractor to make contractual claims should they be actually implemented. Direct loss and/or expense may be involved in prolongation, as well as for any disruption incurred because the regular progress of the works has been disturbed.

Clause 4.12.7 is very important since it not only deals with the question of variations but also with their cumulative effect. Normally, most Contractors realise that the valuation of variations is fairly straightforward but it is the cumulative effect of large numbers of variations which they find cause the real difficulties of disruption and delay.

The commentaries to clauses 2.4.1 to 2.4.14 should be read in conjunction with clauses 4.12.1 to 4.12.7. The correlation between the two sets of clauses is not identical since, for example, clause 2.4.5 includes postponement but under clause 4.12.5 it is given as a separate listing from clause 4.12.7.

General remarks on contractual claims
Clause 53(1) of the GC/Works/1-Edition 2 form of contract refers to 'results in the regular progress of the Works ... being materially disrupted or prolonged'. It can be wondered why the JCT was not equally specific and precise in its terminology.

Prolongation and disruption are the two major contractual claims on normal contracts, as far as lump sums of finance are concerned. There is also the negative claim of allowing an extension of time without any financial liability for the Employer but nevertheless allowing the Contractor to escape from liquidated damages. This should be the very least that the Contractor should attempt in the field of 'claims'.

Further, should the Contractor be unable to obtain an extension of time because the whole works have not been delayed, he may still have a contractual claim for disruption where clause 4.12 is not influenced by clause 2.4 and stands financially on its own.

Disturbance
The noun 'disturbance' is presumably used by legal draughtsmen in preference to the more definitive (usual) noun 'disruption'. However, disruption is used generally by the protagonists in the settlement of claims for extensions of time, as well as for direct loss and/or expense arising from prolongation and disruption to the regular progress to the works. The English noun 'disturbance' is derived from the French and according to Chambers Twentieth Century Dictionary is derived from two roots to 'agitate' and 'a crowd' and is further defined 'to throw into confusion'.

Clause for extension of time	Description of event	Clause for payment	Related causes
2.4.1	Force majeure	—	—
2.4.2	Exceptionally adverse weather conditions	—	—
2.4.3	Loss or damage to the works caused by any one or more of the special perils:		
	(i) Clause 6.3A	(i) 6.3A	6.3 Perils Payment by the contractors's insurance company
	(ii) Clause 6.3B	(ii) 6.3B	By employer's insurance company
	(iii) Clause 6.3C	(iii) 6.3C	Ditto
2.4.4	Civil commotion, local combination of workmen, strike or lock-out, etc.	—	—
2.4.5	Postponement	4.12.5	3.15
2.4.5	Compliance with architect's instructions	4.12.7	1.4,1.7,3.3,3.6,3.8, 5.2,5.4
2.4.6	Opening up or testing for work in accordance with the contract	4.12.2	3.12,3.13.1, 3.14
2.4.7	Not receiving necessary instructions, drawings or details in due time	4.12.1	1.7,3.6,3.6, 3.6.2
2.4.8	Non-contractural work by the employer or others	4.12.3	3.11
2.4.9	Supply of materials or goods by the employer	4.12.4	—
2.4.10	Inability to obtain labour by the contractor for reasons beyond his control	—	—
2.4.11	Inability to obtain materials or goods by the contractor for reasons beyond his control	—	—
2.4.12	Failure by the employer to give in due time ingress or egress from the site	4.12.6	—
2.4.13	Carrying out by a local authority or statutory undertaker in work pursuant to its statutory obligations	—	Clauses 5.1, 5.2, 5.3
2.4.14	Deferment of the possession of the site by the employer if clause 2.2 operates	4.11(a)	Clause 2.2. This is an alternative clause
2.4.15	If SMM7 is used, for approximate quantities which was not a reasonable forecast in the contract bills	4.12.8	Only applicable if SMM7 is used

Table 3.3 CORRELATION BETWEEN CLAUSE 2.4 AND 4.12

When a Contractor claims disturbance to the regular progress of the works or part thereof, whether or not it relates to a prolongation for which there have been agreed extensions of time with financial liability by the Employer and/or a claim for disruption of the labour force and plant, he must be in a strong position to prove every detail of his claim to the Architect or the Quantity Surveyor. Under English law it is essential to deal with the burden of proof, meeting the civil standard of proof as explained previously. Also, the burden or onus of proof must carry the necessary corroborative evidence. As a general rule, it is imperative for the burden or onus of proof to rest with the person who asserts an affirmative statement in a contractual claim. Should the Contractor appear to have discharged his duty in this regard, then legally the burden or onus of proof then shifts from the Contractor to the Architect or Quantity Surveyor to refute the claim! The Contractor should be well informed over the law of evidence and understand the nature of corroboration. The proof and corroboration of evidence cannot be left to vague statements about 'anyone can see disruption on this contract without any help from me' or 'I have lost a fortune on this contract and must obviously be entitled to a substantial claim for disturbance' or 'I have been bothered and bewildered from start to finish as well as from pillar to post'.

Amendment A of IFC84 requires the following alteration when SMM7 is employed in the preparation of the contract bills:

Clause 4.12.1 After instructions add '(*including those for or in regard to the expenditure of provisional sums).*'
Clause 4.12.7 After clause 3.8 quoted in clause 4.12.7 add: '*except where the Contract Documents include bills of quantities, for the expenditure of a provisional sum for defined work included in such Bills.*' An asterisk against work refers to a footnote to clause 8.3 (Definitions).

Clause 4.12.8 Is an additional ground for direct loss and/or expense should there be disturbance to the regular progress of the Works or part thereof, as follows: '*The execution of work for which an Approximate Quantity is included in the Contract Documents which is not a reasonably accurate forecast of the quantity of work required.*'

Table 3.3 gives the correlation between clauses 2.4.1 to 2.4.15 and clauses 4.12.1. to 4.12.8.

CONDITION 5 - STATUTORY OBLIGATIONS, ETC.
Clause 5.1 - Statutory obligations, notices,fees and charges.
Clause 5.1 is very far-ranging in requiring the Contractor to '*comply with and give all notices required by any statute, any statutory instrument, rule or order or any regulation or bye-law applicable to the Works ...*'

Whilst the Contractor has to first of all pay all fees and charges in respect of the works they are contractually and legally recoverable under the second paragraph of clause 5.1, ie '*The amount of any such fees or charges (including any (local authority) rates or taxes other than Value Added Tax) shall be added to the Contract Sum - unless they are required by the Specification, Schedules of Works, Contract Bills to be included in the Contract Sum.*' (Note clause 4.2.2 in regard to clause 5.1.)

Clause 5.2 - Notice of divergence from statutory requirements.
Clause 5.2 requires the Contractor to inform the Architect immediately by means of a written notice specifying the divergence.

Clause 5.3 - Extent of the Contractor's liability for non-compliance.

Clause 5.3 can relieve the Contractor of any liability for any work which does not comply with the statutory requirement where, and to the extent, that such non-compliance of the works results from the Contractor having carried out work in accordance with the contract documents or any instruction of the Architect. Clause 5.3 is, however, subject to clause 5.2.

Clause 5.4 - Emergency compliance.

Clause 5.4 deals with the situation when an emergency occurs where the Contractor may be required to supply materials or execute work before receiving instructions from the Architect.

Clause 5.4.1 states '*the Contractor shall supply such limited materials and execute such limited work as are reasonably necessary to secure immediate compliance with the Statutory Requirements.*'

Clause 5.4.1 requires the Contractor to inform the Architect immediately thereof presumably with full details and particulars or orders from the statutory authority.

Clause 5.4.3 states '*the work and materials shall be treated as if they had been executed and supplied pursuant to an Architect's instruction requiring a variation issued in accordance with clause 3.6 (Variations), provided that the Contractor has informed the Architect in accordance with clause 5.4.2 and the emergency arose because of a divergence between the Statutory Requirements and all or any of the following documents namely: The Contract Document or the Specification of the Schedules of Work or the Contract Bills, or any instruction or any drawing or document issued by the Architect under clauses 1.7 (Further drawings or details), 3.5 (Architect's Instruction) or 3.9 (Levels).*'

It is surprising that such a detailed clause only provides payment to the Contractor in the sole case of an emergency which occurs due to a divergence between the statutory requirements and the contract documents as listed. It can only be surmised that all other emergencies are the subject of the all risks insurance policy required under clauses 6.3A or 6.3B or 6.3C or liability under clauses 6.1.1 to 6.2.5.

Clause 5.5 - Value added tax: Supplemental Condition A

Clause 5.5 correlates to the second Article and makes clear that the Contractor's contract sum is exclusive of VAT. As and when any VAT becomes payable, it will be added to the contract rates and prices.

Clause 5.6 - Statutory tax deduction scheme: Supplemental Condition B

Clause 5.6 states that '*Where at the Base Date the Employer was a Contractor, or where at any time up to the issue and payment of the final certificate for payment the Employer becomes a 'Contractor' for the purposes of the statutory tax deduction scheme referred to in Supplemental Condition B, that Condition shall be operated.*' It follows, therefore, for the purpose of the statutory deduction scheme, that the Employer becomes a Contractor, the Contractor becomes a Sub-contractor and a Sub-contractor becomes a Sub-sub-contractor. In this instance reference should be made to clause 8.2.

CONDITION 7 - DETERMINATION
Condition 7 sets out the various grounds for determining the employment of the Contractor under the contract:

Clause 7.1 Determination by the Employer.

Clause 7.2 Contractor becoming bankrupt, etc.

Clause 7.3 Corruption: determination by Employer.

Clause 7.4 Consequences of determination under clauses 7.1 to 7.3.

Clause 7.5 Determination by Contractor.

Clause 7.6 Employer becoming bankrupt.

Clause 7.7 Consequences of determination under clauses 7.5 and 7.6.

Clause 7.8.1 Determination by Employer or Contractor.

The opportunity or grounds for the Contractor to determine his employment under the contract is covered under clauses 2.4.1 to 2.4.14.

CONDITION 8 - INTERPRETATION, etc.

Condition 8 devolves into five clauses:

Clause 8.1 Reference to clauses, etc.

Clause 8.2 Articles, etc., to be read as a whole.

Clause 8.3 Definitions.

Clause 8.4 Definition of the Architect or alternatively the contract administrator.

Clause 8.5 Priced specification or priced schedules of work.

Clause 8.2 - Articles, etc., to be read as a whole.
A good example of an exclusion as to the meaning of proper names under clause 8.2 is given in clause 5.6 where it will have been seen that the Employer becomes the Contractor, the Contractor the Sub-contractor and the Sub-contractor the Sub-sub-contractor.

Clause 8.3 - Definition
Under clause 8.3 reference is made to various definitions in the contract. The definition of the

contract sum analysis (see the second Recital) means an analysis by the Contractor in accordance with the stated requirements of the Employer. Should there not be a *'stated requirement'*, then the Contractor is free to present the contract sum analysis in any form he chooses. The second Article also refers to a schedule of rates (supplied by the Contractor but not defined in clause 8.3).

The distinction between the definition of *'excepted risks'* and *'specified perils'* should be distinguished.

'Schedules of work' is an unpriced schedule referring to the works, which has been provided by the Employer and which, if priced by the Contractor (as mentioned in the second Recital) for the computation of the contract sum, is included in the contract documents.

However, there is no attempt in the contract to define the schedule of rates to be submitted by the Contractor to the Employer under the second Recital - Alternative 'B'. The contract sum analysis is, as has already been discussed, given a definition in clause 8.3 so why not define the schedule of rates to be supplied by the Contractor? Without such a definition it would be difficult to refuse to accept the Contractor's submission however it might be presented.

Clause 8.4 - Architect/The contract administrator
It was stated earlier that the noun 'Architect' would be chosen in preference to 'the contract administrator'.

Clause 8.5 - Priced specification or priced schedules of work
Clause 8.5 states, *'Where in the Conditions there is a reference to the 'Specification' or the 'Schedules of Work' then, where the 2nd Recital Alternative 'A' applies, such reference is to the Specification or the Schedules of Work as priced by the Contractor unless the context otherwise requires.'*

Under Condition 8 the fourth amendment to IFC84 requires two definitions to clause 8.3 to be added if SMM7 is to be used. The first amendment is:

'Approximate Quantity: means a quantity in the Contract Documents identified therein as an approximate quantity.'

A footnote to this amendment draws attention to the General Rules 10.1 to 10.6 of SMM7 and then quotes the clauses themselves.

The second amendment is:

'Provisional Sum: where the Contract Documents include bills of quantities, includes a sum provided in such bills for work whether defined or undefined work.'

CONDITION 9 - SETTLEMENT OF DISPUTES - ARBITRATION
Condition 9 consists of eight clauses setting out the principles of procedure for arbitration. Clause 4.11, last paragraph, gives the Contractor the alternative of litigation.

Instructions, notices, consents and ascertainments

Various clauses in the contract refer to instructions by the Architect, notices to be given to the Employer, the Architect or the Contractor, consents by the Employer or the Contractor, as well as ascertainments by either the Architect or the Quantity Surveyor when so instructed by the Architect and Table 3.4 lists most of those clauses concerned:

Table 3.4 Clauses relating to instructions, notices, consents and ascertainments

Instruction clauses	1.4	3.7	5.2	
	2.2	3.7.8	5.3	
	2.4.14	3.8	5.4	
	2.10	3.9	5.4.3	
	3.3.1	3.12	6.2.4	
	3.3.2	3.13.1	6.3B.3(b)	
	3.3.3	3.13.2	6.3C.3(b)	
	3.3.4	3.14	6.3C.3(c)	
	3.3.5	3.15	7.4(a)	
	3.3.6	4.5	7.4(b)	
	3.5.1	4.12.1	7.5.3(a)	
	3.5.2	4.12.5	7.5.3(b)	
	3.6	4.12.7		
Notices clauses	2.2	6.3A.3	7.1(d)	B 5.1
	2.7	6.3B.2	7.5	
	3.3.3	6.3B.3	7.5.3(d)	
	3.13.2	6.3C.1	7.6	
	4.11	6.3C.2	7.8.1	
	4.12.6	6.3C.2(b)	7.8.2	
	5.1	6.3C.2(c)	A 3.2	
	5.2			
	6.2.2	6.3c.3	A 4.4	
	6.3a.2	7.1(c)	A 8	
Consents	1.10	3.1	3.2.2(d)	
	1.11	3.2	3.9	
	4.2.1(c)	3.2.2(a)	3.11	
Ascertainments	3.7	4.2	4.11	
	3.7.7	4.2.2	7.4(d)	
	3.13.2	4.5	7.7(b)	

4. Final Accounts

The final account to a building contract is vital in the pursuit of contractual claims since it will reveal many of the fundamental facts generic to the founding of claims. The philosophy of some Contractors is not to seek a thoroughly investigated final account but to rely solely on the creation of claims. This philosophy is unsound since it may not allow full understanding of the significance of the nature of changes to the contract, whereas an exhaustive examination of the facts is absolutely imperative to the settlement of the final account.

A fertile source of claims arises from the proliferation of Architect's instructions for variations, which may demonstrate to the Contractor that the project he had tendered for has become an almost entirely different building. Most arbitration or litigation is predominantly concerned with the issue of variations or their failure to be issued. The facts can only be revealed by time and skill spent in examining the history and chronology of the contract from start to finish. Maria Callas said the opera does not commence with the raising of the theatre curtain or finish with the lowering of the curtain. This is equally true of building contracts, where there may well be crucial decisions between the Contractor submitting his original tender and discussions with the Employer until his tender is accepted and the contract is made. The contract does not end when the practical completion is reached, since there may be much negotiation from that point in time until the final account and all the contractual claims have been made, with even then the possibility of arbitration or litigation. Although the contractual responsibility for preparing the final account is that of the Quantity Surveyor, it is a contractual requirement for the Contractor to submit all documents reasonably required for the purposes of the final account.

The Contractor should always be in contact with the Quantity Surveyor, by providing the necessary notices for all star items and star rates and keeping him fully informed over all the issues which attract different rates and prices to those in the contract bills. Unless the Quantity Surveyor under the contract is resident on the site he cannot be aware of the detail of the day-to-day problems of the contract and thereby ensure proper reimbursement is made to the Contractor. It is quite possible that the Quantity Surveyor will require confirmation of the issues which the Contractor may raise and suitable site arrangements should be made by the Contractor to facilitate such confirmation.

The following list of points to be made concerning the preparation of the final account may also successfully provide the information and data required for the granting of any extensions of time and the grounds caused thereby for contractual claims for delay, disturbance, dislocation and disruption. This also involves the Contractor in fully analysing the final account to demonstrate the power and extent of his arguments. An example of this analysis is given later in this publication. Nothing is more disappointing and as unprofitable as the Contractor sitting silent at a meeting to attempt to obtain extension of time awards and being totally unable to prove his argument from his knowledge of the facts in the final account. Unfortunately, this happens from time to time. Not to view the final account as a key document is to court financial disaster.

Some of the vital points which the Contractor should consider when concerned with the preparation of the final account and issues arising therefrom are:

(1) a full examination of all the pre-contract correspondence and any signed documents which can influence the final account. Ensure all interim agreements are legally incorporated into the actual contract;

(2) an examination of the actual site itself to ensure that the contract drawings have correctly shown the boundaries and any existing buildings and that all levels given are correct. All anomalies to be agreed before work is commenced;

(3) photograph the existing site in detail before the works commence. It is very important to be able to demonstrate that which existed before the works or any variations have been executed;

(4) record and agree any dumping of refuse on the site between tendering and commencing the contract. Similarly, determine whether the Employer has changed the site in any way, such as covering it with a layer of fly-ash or other materials, etc.;

(5) record any flooding on the site and subsequently ensure that all the water table levels are recorded at the time of their being discovered with the Architect or clerk of works in accordance with the SMM;

(6) ensure that all work which will be covered up has been agreed prior to its execution, such as excavation depths for foundations, pier or column bases, basements, ground beams, drainage trenches, manholes, external works and the like. Also all soft spots as well as the nature of the filling material to the soft spots, breaking out of hard substances such as concrete, reinforced concrete, masonry, brickwork, tarmacadam, piling, timber, should be recorded and agreed at the time of their execution;

(7) accurate cost records should be made and agreed concerning all pumping and paling of water below water table level down to the bottom depth of the excavation;

(8) record details of all works-on-site items required by the Architect and agree at the time of their execution;

(9) remeasure all the work concerned in provisional sums relating to the Main Contractor;

(10) remeasure all provisional quantities and obtain signed records necessary for their subsequent agreement;

(11) prepare all 'as built' drawings to prove facts concerning any later items of possible dispute generally and also in regard to 'builders work in connection with all specialist trades' by Sub-contractors;

(12) keep an up-to-date register of all changes in the contract drawings by the issue of further drawings and details as well as variations. It is much more economic to do this task on a day-to-day basis at the time of their occurrence than leave it until the end of the contract. Actual site staff working at the time of occurrences can often highlight important facts and issues and this vital benefit should not be lost by delays;

(13) at the same time the Contractor should read all the correspondence, site diaries, clerk of works' reports, recorded telephone messages and other relevant documents and take active steps to ensure payment for any adverse circumstances (not the fault of the Contractor) and pursue the issues until a resolution one way or the other is obtained. Ensure that for every letter received or sent, a reply is obtained;

(14) give prior notice before commencing any work on a variation if star items and star rates are being sought. To apply months after executing variations for star items and star rates will be met by the argument 'You proceeded without protesting and, therefore, cannot expect at this late stage to receive enhanced rates.' However unfair this argument may appear it can always be overcome by applying for star items and star rates before commencing any variations;

(15) similarly, due notice must be given if the Contractor intends to seek a daywork basis of payment for a variation;

(16) the Contractor must check all drawings, including bar bending schedules, carefully to discover any errors, inconsistencies, divergences or omissions and apply for the relevant correction or variation;

(17) the Contractor must also carefully check the contract bills for errors, inconsistencies, divergences, omissions or any departures from the SMM;

(18) keep accurate cost records of any variations involving new materials or processes or labour content and plant because there are no germane rates and prices in the contract to assist the agreement of star items and star rates;

(19) never carry out any variation whatsoever without the prior receipt of a written instruction from the Architect;

(20) walk round the entire works every day and investigate any item which appears to be executed differently from the contract. In particular, find out the reasons why any new work is now being demolished and decide whose fault it is and take the appropriate action;

(21) constantly remind the Architect when information is still outstanding and record when the information is late, very late or even too late;

(22) prepare a 'goods in' abstract and check individual quantities against the final account quan-

tities and seek reimbursement for omissions, shortfall or shortages;

(23) if any items have been especially made for the works, such as a staircase balustrade, which is subsequently omitted, seek reimbursement because the balustrade now only has a scrap metal value and not its original cost;

(24) seek reimbursement from Sub-contractors for any labour, material or plant supplied at their request and for their use;

(25) ensure that all invoices for materials, goods, plant, plant hire and scaffolding are retained safely for subsequent negotiations;

(26) photograph any contentious items, since the vision of an item can be much more certain by a photograph than by volumes of correspondence;

(27) be very determined to be paid at the contract times since there is always the possibility that these payments may slide during the currency of the contract. Ensure that the release of retentions is made at the correct time;

(28) seek to resolve all financial issues with Sub-contractors or merchants before seeking reimbursement with the Quantity Surveyor;

(29) register in writing all claims for delays and disturbance at their time of occurrence;

(30) contra-charge all Sub-contractors or suppliers for delays and disturbance caused by them;

(31) always question whether a star item and star rate is necessary and not just accept contract rates and prices for the sake of peace and quiet;

(32) similarly, it is always necessary to question when omissions are involved should the total rates in the contract bills be omitted or an adjustment made which is against the Contractor's interest;

(33) also question whether work is executed under the same conditions or of similar character or has there been a significant change in the quantities set out in the work set out in the 'priced document';

(34) are any additional preliminary items involved over and above the contract rates and prices?;

(35) when substantial omissions are incurred does the remaining work need star items and star rates because of these omissions?;

(36) is daywork being executed out of sequence or have there been any alterations (by variations) concerning limitations on the site accesses or working areas or working hours?;

(37) is there any excessive waste of, or deterioration to, materials due to contractual delays by the Employer or Architect?;

(38) has very long delay caused plant to become obsolete?;

(39) has the Employer failed to supply goods or materials on time or not at all?;

(40) has there been any discovery of fossils, antiquities or other objects of value and what effect did this have on the contract?

Lump sum contracts
A lump sum contract only requires the contract sum to be adjusted in accordance with contract conditions and may consist of the following items:

(a) variations;
(b) daywork;
(c) Named Sub-contractors;
(d) provisional sums;
(e) contingencies;
(f) provisional quantities;
(g) clauses.

This may result in a very simple financial statement to be given in the final certificate, perhaps as follows:

	£
Amount of the contract sum	= 409,116
Less omissions	= 110,784
	298,332
Add additions including daywork and price fluctuations	= 353,664
TOTAL of Final Account	= £651,996

These brief details do not demonstrate properly the real nature of the contract and the changes which have taken place during the currency of the contract and the possible financial effect which is likely to arise. Neither do they give assistance in preparing contractual claims.

The analysis of the final account given in Figure 4.1 seeks to establish incontrovertible proof of the need for granting extensions of time and the nature of the disturbance to the regular progress of the works which attracts direct loss and/or expense under clause 4.11.

Figure 4.1 clearly sets out the most important changes in the contract and should be capable of

Items adjusted in the contract sum:	Final account value		Commentary
	Omissions	Additions	
1. Contingencies	20000	—	Contingencies must always be omitted
2. Variations (omissions) valued under clause 3.7.2	16910	—	Omissions valued at contract rates
3. Variations (omissions) not valued under clause 3.7.2	10811		See reasons given under the commentary to clause 3.7.2
4. Variation (additions) valued under clauses 3.7.3 and 3.7.6	—	19010	Additions valued at contract rates
5. Variations (additions) valued under clause 3.7.3 whilst of a similar character are not carried out under similar conditions	—	15999	Consideration for due allowance added to contract rates. Note clause 3.7.8
6. Variations (additions) valued under clauses 3.7.3 and 3.7.6 whilst of a similar character and conditions but having a significant change in quantity	—	11566	Consideration for due allowance made to contract rates
7. Variations (additions) valued partially under clause 3.7.3 whilst of a similar character but not of a similar condition and with a significant change in quality	—	9787	Consideration for due allowance made to contract rates
8. Variations (omissions) not valued under clauses 3.7.4 and 3.7.3 and which are not of a similar character	8147	—	Omissions not valued at contract rates but at a fair valuation
9. Variations (additions) not valued under clauses 3.7.4 or 3.3.7 and which are not of a similar character	—	19117	Additions not valued at contract rates but at a fair valuation
10. Variations (additions) not value under clauses 3.7.4 or 3.7.3 for substituted work and not of a similar character	—	4718	Additions not valued at contract rates but at a fair valuation
11. Daywork under clause 3.7.5 as ordered by the architect: (a) Performing new work (b) Demolishing new work (c) Re-building after demolition (d) Restitution of work ordered to be tested and found to be in accordance with the contract, including demolition and removal of debris from the site and then re-executing the work (e) Sundry builders work in connection with specialists which needed revision	— — — — —	7885 9386 13689 5819 12227	Appropriate basis for a fair valuation and valued at the prime cost definition for the main contractor as well as for the heating and electrical at their own definition of prime cost for specialists
12. Breaking out existing brickwork, concrete, reinforced concrete, items excavated during the execution of foundations, drainage and external works.	4866	16551	N.B. Whilst there were only 781 rates in the contract bills in the final account 1998 star items and star rates were found necessary
13. Disposal of ground water tables discovered during excavation	—	14114	

FIGURE 4.1 Final account analysis

110

(Fig 4.1 continued)

14. Work required by the architect to be executed out of sequence or otherwise affected by other variations	–	17335	Note clauses 3.6.2 and 3.7.8
15. Errors found in the contract bills	–	8787	
16. Inconsistencies discovered in the contract documents	–	11817	
17. Shortages	–	6976	
18. Adjustment of provisional quantities	9434	22472	
19. Overtime ordered by the architect	–	17418	
20. Adjustment of named sub-contractors	15616	48227	Contract became more complicated due to the addition of
21. Provisional sums for defined work	18000	22874	(a) Internal phones
22. Provisional sums for un-defined work	7000	11223	(b) External telecom phones
23. Price fluctuations	–	26667	(c) Air conditioning (d) Computer lines
TOTALS	110784	353664	

demonstrating, beyond doubt, the prolongation and disturbance to the regular progress of the works and the consequential direct loss and/or expense.

The Contractor is now equipped to attend meetings and prove on the balance of probabilities the reason for his requirement of extensions of time and the nature of disturbance. Without such an analysis of the contract finances the Contractor would find it very difficult to argue successfully.

In regard to variations it is their proliferation which is so important, since it is their cumulative effect that causes disturbance to the regular progress of the works. In this regard by analogy it is far better to have a 'bushel of cherries' rather than one 'large water melon'.

Essential elements of the final account
Over and above the day-to-day search for variations it is very important to realise that there are three essential elements to be used by the Contractor when measuring variations and these are:

(i) correct quantity;
(ii) correct description;
(iii) correct rate or price.

(i) Correct quantity
Whilst it is not expressly stated in the contract that the Contractor is to meet the Quantity Surveyor for the purposes of agreeing the valuation of variations, as is required in other JCT building contracts, it is clearly inferential from clause 4.5, which requires the Contractor to provide the Quantity Surveyor with all documents reasonably required for the adjustment of the contract sum.

The Contractor will be allowed to discuss all the financial issues of the contract with the Quantity Surveyor which will enable the Contractor to present his arguments for star items and star rates. (Note also the relevance of clause 4.7.)

It is obvious that the Contractor will know in detail what has happened during the currency of the contract on a day-to-day basis and he must then either inform the Quantity Surveyor directly or, alternatively, the Architect of the need for star items and star rates. If the Contractor presents his arguments directly to the Quantity Surveyor it eventually follows that the Architect will be asked by the Quantity Surveyor to confirm or deny the Contractor's arguments. Under clause 3.7 the contract provides for the Contractor to agree the valuation of variations, provisional sums and provisional quantities directly with the Employer - although this seems a most unlikely course to be taken by the Employer since he has appointed the Architect and the Quantity Surveyor to act on his behalf. The Employer would not be expected to have a sound working knowledge of the SMM. It is open to the Employer to discuss and agree the financial arrangements which he occasioned, if he wished to accelerate his contract but, nevertheless, he would prudently seek professional advice from his Architect and Quantity Surveyor.

On the basis that the Quantity Surveyor and the Contractor regularly meet to discuss the final account measurement, it is fundamentally important for the Contractor to have a wide experience and knowledge of using the SMM, as well as a background understanding of the various issues and risks which are associated with the SMM procedures, including various documents concerned with the SMM.

The SMM can be very useful in establishing whether the Contractor is entitled to an item or items of measurement for quantities, since the quantity itself must be first decided.

For instance, if a variation for a reinforced concrete wall is issued by an instruction from the Architect, the SMM decides it will be measured as a cubic quantity and requires a superficial formwork to be measured to its vertical faces and a tonnage given of the rod reinforcement specified.

If the contract bills had not measured formwork to the vertical faces of a reinforced concrete wall, then the SMM could give the proof that it should be measured as set out in clauses 1.4 and 1.5 of the contract. Similarly, if the rod reinforcement had not been measured in the contract bills, the SMM can give the requisite proof.

The SMM requires the contract bills to give a list of the drawings from which the bills of quantities have been prepared and which will be available for inspection by the Contractor. Therefore, one of the first tasks the Contractor must accomplish is to compare those taking-off drawings with the contract drawings to discover whether there is any difference between the two sets. Presumably it is then the responsibility of the Contractor to draw the Quantity Surveyor's attention to those differences and to obtain the variation instructions necessary to reconcile any differences between the two sets of drawings under clauses 1.4 and 1.7.

Another possible source of error can arise if the Quantity Surveyor, when preparing the contract bills, employs the wrong scale rule for a particular drawing detail. If instead of using the correct scale of 1 in 20 a scale of 1 in 10 is used, then the error for lineal items would be twice, for superficial items it would be four times and for cubic items it would be eight times too small. In such an event the comparison of the billed quantities with a 'goods in' abstract might well originate an investigation, bringing such errors to the notice of the Contractor. The Contractor should never finally agree a quantity for an item whilst there is a doubt about its accuracy. Instead, the proferred quantity should be only provisionally accepted until a final resolution is agreed. Some of the possible contract clauses concerned with the measurement of quantities are: 1.1, 1.2, 1.4, 1.5, 1.7, 1.10, 1.11, 2.1, 2.2, 2.3, 2.4, 2.9, 2.10, 3.5.1, 3.5.2, 3.6, 3.7, 3.8, 3.9, 3.11, 3.12, 3.14, 3.15, 4.1, 4.5, 4.6, 4.7, 4.9, 4.10, 4.11, 4.12, 5.1, 5.3, 5.4, 6.1.1 to 6.3D.4, 7.5, 7.8.1, 8.3, 9.1 to 9.8 and Article 5.

(ii) Correct description

A very important part of valuing variations is to ensure that the correct description is obtained by the Contractor from the Quantity Surveyor. If the Contractor just accepts the description in the contract bills he will only receive bill rates and prices, which may not be the case. The change in the description may be to the item itself but, equally, could relate to a heading which also changes and affects the valuation of many other items. Such headings could be:

(i) variations not executed under the same conditions;
(ii) variations with a significant change in quantity;
(iii) variations not executed under the same conditions and also having a significant change in quantity;
(iv) variations not of the same character as that of the contract itself;
(v) variations invoking additional preliminaries which are to be included in the star items and star rates;
(vi) variations which substantially change the conditions under which any other work is executed.

The need for a heading for star items and star rates can arise when ordinary foundation work becomes the subject of underpinning, or when the sequential order of the contract is changed by a variation, or when one or more accesses are closed by the Employer under clause 3.6.2, or because of specified perils. The Contractor should not agree to a description until he is totally satisfied. He can, for interim certificate purposes only, agree the description provisionally, leaving final agreement to later.

Clauses related to the description of items are: 1.1, 1.2, 1.4, 1.5, 1.7, 1.10, 1.11, 2.10, 3.5.1, 3.5.2, 3.6, 3.7, 3.8, 3.9, 3.11, 3.12, 3.14, 4.5, 4.6, 4.7, 4.9, 4.10, 4.11, 4.12, 5.1, 5.2, 5.3, 5.4, 6.1.1 to 6.3D.4, 7.5, 7.8.1, 8.3, 9.1 to 9.8 and Article 5.

The three elements of correct quantity, description and rate or price are equal to each other and dependent onc upon the other at one level of consideration. However, at another level the correct description is predominant over the other two, since it can allow the Contractor to obtain higher rates and prices than those he might have been offered in the contract bills.

(iii) Correct rate or price

A vital part of valuing variations is to obtain the correct rate or price, whether a contract price or a star rate. As already stated one important element in achieving star rates is to have obtained a description for the item involved in the variation which allows the Contractor, by virtue of the change in description, to obtain star rates in lieu of contract rates. It would be a pointless to negotiate the correct quantity and the correct description and then to throw it all away by accepting an incorrect rate. This can easily be done by not taking care to research the item fully and by not having accurate cost records to support the claim for the star rate. The value is stressed of agreeing rates provisionally until the full facts and cost data have been obtained and the correct rate finally agreed. Failure to do so can have serious financial consequences. Obviously, the Contractor should never allow junior staff to engage in rate fixing. The clauses concerned with correct rates and prices include: 1.1, 1.2, 1.4, 1.5, 1.7, 1.10, 1.11, 2.10, 3.5.1, 3.5.2, 3.6, 3.7 to 3.8, 3.9, 3.11, 3.12, 3.14, 4.5, 4.6, 4.7, 4.9, 4.10, 4.11, 4.12, 5.1, 5.2, 5.3, 5.4, 6.1.1 to 6.3D.4, 7.5, 7.8.1, 8.3, 9.1 to 9.8 and Article 5.

Overheads

If the Architect makes substantial changes in the choice of the kind or standard of materials and goods it is inevitable that the Contractor's head office will incur additional costs. Unless detailed particulars are kept, some difficulty may occur in proving such extra cost. In such circumstances the following formula may assist in obtaining payment for the extra cost of overheads:

(ADDITIONS + OMISSIONS) - (ADDITIONS - OMISSIONS) X A%

Using the figures given in the example of a final account which has an additions figure of £353,664 and an omissions figure of £110,784, the total of additions and omissions will be:

$$£353,664$$
$$\underline{£110,784}$$
$$\underline{£464,448}$$

The result of deducting the omissions from the additions will be a gain:

$$£353,664$$
$$\underline{£110,784}$$
$$\underline{£242,880}$$

The A% will be an agreed head office on-cost related to those matters involved in the cancellation of orders and consequent reordering. Assuming that the head office on-cost is agreed at 0.45% then the financial value will be:

$$(£464,448 - £242,880) \times 0.45\%$$

$$= £221,568 \times 0.45\%$$

$$= \underline{£997.06}$$

The reason that the gain of £242,880 is deducted lies in the fact that the £242,880 value already contains overheads (and profit) whilst the omissions have had their overheads deducted. The formula recognises the need to consider the total of the value of the additions and the omissions, since both involve head office on-costs. The contractual grounds for this claim arise out of clause 4.12.7 which contemplates the cumulative effect of variations as far as expense is concerned.

Materials on site

A very comprehensive record of all materials delivered to the site for incorporation into the works must be kept and up-dated as necessary. When materials are actually incorporated into the works they must be deleted from the list in part or in whole, dependent upon whether they are totally consumed or not. If they are not totally consumed then an investigation is needed to discover why! For instance, they could have been over-measured by the Contractor's purchasing department. Again, the ordering may have been originally correct but, due to subsequent variations, is now reduced in quantity through no fault of the Contractor and invoking the principle of shortfall. If the quantity of material delivered is insufficient there must be an explanation, which could possibly be a shortage in the contract bills.

As to whether the final account is correct may be investigated in the case of, say, concrete produced on the site, as follows:

		m^3
1.	Volume of wet site produced Concrete delivered around site and hoisted into position	30000
2.	Wet volume reduced by setting, consolidation and shrinkage assessed at 40%	$\dfrac{12000}{18000}$
3.	Waste and spillage assessed at 15%	2700
4.	Add volume of concrete disposal by rod reinforcement assessed at 2%	306
		$= \underline{\underline{15606m^3}}$

If the total volume of the concrete measured in the final account has a similar volume of say 15600m³ the Contractor may be satisfied with the result. If there is a wide discrepancy, then further investigation will be necessary. The example is simplified to the extent that the various mixes or strengths of the concrete have not been considered but the same principles would apply equally to each mix or strength of concrete.

Final Account - generally

The various principles examined in regard to final accounts should encourage the Contractor to research the contract thoroughly in every respect to ensure the fullest payment for the works. If the various issues are researched at the time of their occurrence the cost will be at a minimum, whereas if left until the maintenance period they may not only cost more but the actual site staff involved at the time of occurrence may no longer be available and their knowledge perhaps lost for ever!

5. CONTRACTUAL CLAIMS

Only the Architect and Quantity Surveyor can ascertain financial claims arising specifically from contract clauses. All other remaining claims for breaches of contract (not covered by contract claim clauses) are dealt with under the last paragraph of clause 4.11. Table 5.1 lists the various clauses which deal with claims:

Table 5.1 List of clauses that mention or infer claims, damages, liability, direct loss and/or expense, direct loss and/or damage.

Article 2	3.11	6.3.2
Article 5	3.12	6.3.3
1.4	3.13	6.3A
1.7	3.14	6.3B
1.10	3.15	6.3C
1.11	4.6	7.1
2.2	4.7	7.2
2.3	4.8	7.3
2.4	4.11	7.4
2.5	4.12	7.5
2.7	5.1	7.6
2.8	5.2	7.7
2.9	5.3	7.8
2.10	5.4.3	7.9
3.3.4(a)	6.1.1	9.1
3.3.4(b)	6.1.2	9.3
3.3.6	6.1.3	9.4
3.5.1	6.2.1	9.5
3.5.2	6.2.3	9.6
3.6	6.2.4	9.7
3.7	6.2.5	9.8
3.9	6.3.1	

Correlation of contract claim clauses

Contract claim clauses do not stand in splendid isolation from one or another. Their correlation , whether or not the relevant clauses are in themselves a precise claim clause, will assist in preparing a claim. For instance, whilst clause 2.4.8 - extension of time - is not of itself a contact claim clause, it can be linked to clause 4.12.3 which allows for the payment of direct loss and/or expense for the disturbance of the regular progress of the works or part of the works being materially affected. It is also important to realise that when ascertainment is made (wholly or in part) it is to be added to the contract sum without deduction of any retention.

Table 5.2 attempts to give the Contractor the appropriate guidance.

Table 5.2 Inter-relationship of contract claim clauses

No.	Heads of claim	Clause of origin	Claim clauses	Extension of time clause	Payment for extension of time and/or disturbance
1	Inconsistencies in or between the contract documents or drawings and documents issued under clause 1.7 (Further drawings or clause 3.9 (levels)	1.4 1.7	3.5.1 3.6 3.7 2.7	2.4.5	4.12.7
2	Any error in description or in quantity or any omission of items in the contract documents or in any one of such documents	1.4 1.7	3.5.1 3.6 3.7 2.7	2.4.5	4.12.7
3	Any error or omission in the particulars provided by the employer of the tender of a person named in accordance with clause 3.3.1 (named sub-contractors)	1.4 1.7 3.3.1	3.5.1 3.6 3.7 2.7	2.4.5	4.12.7
4	Any departure from the method of preparation of the contract bills referred to in clause 1.5	1.4 1.5	3.5.1 3.6 3.7 2.7	2.4.5	4.12.7
5	Deferment of possession by the employer (if applicable)	2.2	2.2 2.7	2.14.4	4.11(a) (no disturbance for deferment of possession)
6	Loss or damage caused by any one or more of the specified perils	2.4.3 8.3	3.5.1 3.6 3.7 6.3B.3.5 2.7	2.4.3 6.3D.1	Payment by Insurance Co 6.3A.4.5, 6.3B.3.2 6.3C.4.1 6.3C.4.2
7	Variations	3.5.1 3.6 3.6.1 3.6.2	3.7 2.7 5.2 5.4.3	2.4.5	4.12.7
8	Provisional sums	3.8	3.7 2.7	2.4.5	4.12.7

(Table 5.2 cont.)

9	Postponement	3.15	3.7 2.7	2.4.5	4.12.5
10	Named sub-contractor variations	3.3	3.7 2.7	2.4.5	4.12.7
11	Tests or inspection ordered but not revealing any fault by the contractor	3.6.1 3.12 3.13.1 3.13.2	3.7 2.7	2.4.6	4.12.2
12	Failure to provide in time necessary instructions, drawings, details or levels	1.7 3.5.1 3.9	3.7 2.7	2.4.7	4.12.1
13	Delay in the execution of work by the employer or others engaged or employed by the employer	3.5.1 3.11	3.7 2.7	2.4.8	4.12.3
14	Failure or delay by the employer to supply materials or goods	3.5.1	3.6 3.7 2.7	2.4.9	4.12.4
15	Failure by the employer to give in due time ingress or egress from the site	3.5.1	3.6 3.7 2.7	2.4.12	4.12.6

NB   There is no reason why clause 4.11(b) matters cannot alternatively be routed through clause 4.11 last paragraph, as breaches of contract by means of either litigation or arbitration.

FINANCIAL CLAIMS FOR PROLONGATION WHICH HAVE THE EMPLOYER'S CONTRACTUAL LIABILITY FOR DIRECT LOSS AND/OR EXPENSE

Prolongation claims
Prolongation claims which have a financial liability for the Employer for direct loss and/or expense can only arise if an extension of time claim has been agreed by the Architect under clause 2.3 to 2.5 and provided those grounds also carry financial liability under clauses 4.11 to 4.12.7. (Note the commentaries previously given under the clauses given above.)

The direct loss and/or expense claim may not be as simple as it first appears because of the varying issues incurred.

It will be observed that whilst extensions of time are given beyond the original completion date, the actual period granted with financial liability for the Employer may apply in part or in whole as is witnessed by the departure of the agent (item 1) six weeks after the original completion date.

By virtue of clause 3.7.6, payment can be made for items of a preliminary nature arising out of variations and by reason of delay within the original contract period, as evidenced by the concrete batching plant (item 4) or pumping (item 5) during the original contract period (as well as during the extension of time) with financial liability for the Employer for item 3 for scaffolding, mainly within the original contract period and only partially into the extension of time period which has financial liability for the Employer.

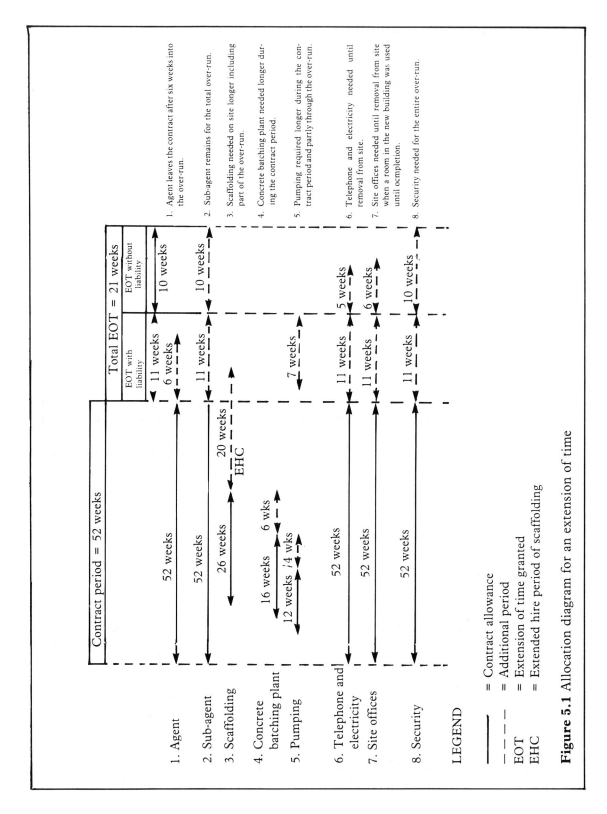

Figure 5.1 Allocation diagram for an extension of time

1. Agent leaves the contract after six weeks into the over-run.

2. Sub-agent remains for the total over-run.

3. Scaffolding needed on site longer including part of the over-run.

4. Concrete batching plant needed longer during the contract period.

5. Pumping required longer during the contract period and partly through the over-run.

6. Telephone and electricity needed until removal from site.

7. Site offices needed until removal from site when a room in the new building was used until ocmpletion.

8. Security needed for the entire over-run.

Example of a prolongation claim

The example given at the Appendix should be regarded as an aide memoir to those matters which the Contractor must address when choosing those items which may apply and which will form an integral part of his claim submission.

Disruption to the regular progress of the works

Delays which may arise during currency of a contract can also incur direct loss and/or expense by reason of disturbance, should the delays be occasioned by the Employer or his Architect and for which they have a contractual and financial liability. Certain changes brought about by the issue of Architect's instructions may also incur disruption.

Such delays and changes may incur:

  (i) disruption;

 (ii) disturbance;

(iii) dislocation;

(iv) disorganisation;

 (v) uneconomic working to the labour force and plant. This in turn may cause some materials with a short life to be wholly or partially wasted due to delays or by deterioration or even evaporation.

Disruption may also occur to a contract which does not have any extensions of time granted by the Architect.

Disruption itself falls into two broad categories:

(a) specific disruption;

(b) general or overall disruption;

(a) Specific disruption
Of the two categories of disruption, ie specific or general, specific disruption is easier to prove.

Specific disruption may incur either partial standing or idle time or complete standing or idle time of operatives.

The standing or idle time may be brought about by the Employer or Architect's instructions for which there is financial liability.

An example could be for another Contractor on an adjacent site, (but not on the contract site) who bursts a high pressure water main which floods the contract foundations and drains to a depth of a metre. In such circumstances the Contractor will have to cease work until the water is removed from his site. The Contractor will then have to record specifically the standing time of his work force whilst the restoration of the site takes place. This should be carried out on a daily basis and submitted to the Architect for corroboration and payment. Of course, the Employer will seek reimbursement from the adjacent Contractor in tort but that is a matter for the Employer and not the Contractor to resolve.

Not all claims for disruption will be as dramatic as this but if on every occasion of delay the Contractor accurately and religiously records all the standing time involved, he may be surprised just how much specific disruption can be successfully accounted for.

Specific disruption can be very important in researching particular areas of the contract which are known for certain to have incurred disruption. For instance, the effect on foundations, drainage and external works by the incidence of an unknown water table to the contracting parties, or the effect of wide ranging variations to the roof perhaps by reason of a change in the Building Regulations.

There is one very successful approach with specific disruption and that is to establish the value of the payment at the time of the occurrence. At that time the claim will be investigated, when the facts and details are still fresh in the minds of the Employer, Contractor, Architect, Quantity Surveyor and the clerk of works. All claims for specific disruption should be sought under clause 4.7 and 4.11.

The Contractor must be careful to segregate specific disruption caused by the Employer and the Architect from any disruption brought about by Named Sub-contractors or domestic Sub-contractor from whom reimbursement must be sought (and not from the Employer).

Similar arguments equally apply to the disruption of plant.

(b) General disruption
General disruption is a very cumbersome concept of a contractual claim due to the disturbance of the general progress of works under clauses 4.7 and 4.11. As has been stated before if the Contractor is required by clause 2.1 'on possession to begin and regularly and diligently proceed with the Works and shall complete the same on or before the Date of Completion stated in the Appendix, subject nevertheless to the provisions for extension of time in clause 2.3' and then the Employer or Architect causes disturbance to the regular progress to the works a claim arises. At the request of the Architect or the Quantity Surveyor the Contractor must in support of his claim submit such information as is reasonably necessary (clause 4.11).

The Contractor may claim that he has lost a considerable sum of money and suggest that this is sufficient evidence in itself of disruption. However, a mere financial loss is not acceptable as proof to a civil standard of proof. Proof is absolutely necessary to establish the grounds of general disruption. It is suggested that the detailed reading of the final account given previously will provide some of the definitive grounds for a disruption claim. In any general claim of disruption it will be argued against the Contractor that the real cause of disruption is because of the failure by the Contractor, domestic Sub-contractor, suppliers, plant hire firms, statutory undertakers to perform economically, as well as poor supervision by the agent and foreman or trade supervisors. All these objections must be overcome to achieve a successful claim. A sound knowledge of all the workings of the contract itself may serve to reveal the actual causes of disruption. This is not an easy task, especially if there are no receptive ears to the Contractor's claim.

In any event the Contractor must be able to demonstrate the credibility and confidence in his arguments to a degree that a Judge may well find 'compelling'. The 'paste and scissors' approach to a claim should never be taken. The Contractor must not become so fascinated by the 'extra-ordinary' that the 'ordinary' is missed entirely. There are limits to what can be claimed under clause 4.11, and the following items are excluded:

(a) variations (clauses 3.6 to 3.7.9);

(b) daywork (clause 3.7.5);

(c) prolongation (clauses 2.2, 2.4, 3.7.6 and 4.11);

(d) bad workmanship or materials or goods (clauses 2.10 and 3.12);

(e) incorrect setting out (clause 3.9);

(f) default by Named Sub-contractor (clauses 3.3.1 to 3.3.8);

(g) lower output by apprentices;

(h) labour already paid for in work out of sequence, dissimilar conditions, dissimilar character, significant change in quantity, omissions of substantial value and resulting changes in remaining conditions after such omissions (clauses 3.6 to 3.7.9);

(i) star items and star rates (clauses 3.6 to 3.7.9);

(j) price fluctuations (clause 4.9) and Supplemental Conditions C and D;

(k) disallowed price fluctuations (clause 4.9 and Supplemental Conditions C or D);

(l) non-productive overtime;

(m) errors and mistakes by the Contractor and Sub-contractors (clause 3.9 and 3.12);

(n) ex-gratia payment (clause 3.7.8);

(o) execution of any work without authorisation (clause 3.5.1 to 3.5.2);

(p) loan of labour, plant, materials and goods to Named Sub-contractors and domestic sub-contrctors;

(q) consequential effect of low or wrong rates or prices in the tender due to under-provision by the Contractor;

(r) labour, plant and materials or goods already paid for by insurers;

(s) idle or uneconomic time lost due to the Contractor's lack of planning and supervisory control.

Since all contracts, to a greater or lesser degree, involve an element of risk this must be taken into consideration when seeking the value of disruption. Therefore, if the value of the contract increases substantially in value then the allowance must also be made in the calculation for that element of risk. If the risk factor was 2% in the contract then an adjustment for this risk must be given in the ensuing calculations. In considering the risk element it is also necessary to provide for the full significance of clause 4.1 of the contract which states that *'the contract sum shall not be adjusted or altered in any way otherwise than in accordance with the express provisions of the Conditions and subject to clause 1.4 (Inconsistencies) any error or omission, whether or arithmetic or not, in the computation of the contract sum shall be deemed to have been accepted by the parties hereto'*.

Apart from these statements the Contractor can only claim for that period of time for which the Employer has actual financial liability, which is normally viewed in proportion to the total extension of time granted to the Contractor by the Architect.

One of the methods for attempting to ascertain the quantum of disruption is that which is based on the total number of hours worked on the contract, including extensions of time, from which is deducted the total hours derived from the final account multiplied by the percentage of the Employer's contractual and financial liability. Due allowance must have been made for all due abatements previously detailed. This is not a 'counsel of perfection' but may well serve to delineate the parameters of the problem.

It follows naturally enough that in the first case, should the total hours worked by the Contractor be less than the total hours found in the final account, there is no apparent proof of disruption. Similarly, in the second case, if the hours worked by the Contractor almost equate to the total hours found in the final account there is no apparent proof of disruption. It is only in the third case where the actual hours worked by the Contractor exceed those total hours in the final account that any disruption argument can arise and then the argument will have to be proved to a civil standard of proof, since loss in itself is not sufficient evidence. This proof is by no means easy to establish but nevertheless it can be successfully achieved. It must be clear that 'any specific disruption' already agreed would need to be deducted from the value of the general disruption claim.

The following illustrates these principles:

EXAMPLE OF AN ASSESSMENT FOR A DISRUPTION CLAIM MADE UNDER CLAUSES 4.7 AND 4.11

		£
Amount of final account		651,996
Less payment to statutory undertakers	19,800	
Preliminaries in the contract	61,000	
Overtime ordered by the Architect	17,418	
Named Sub-contractors	48,227	
Price fluctuations	26,667	
Water and insurance	17,040	190,152
		= 461,844

Less

Overheads and profit at 10%

$$= \frac{£461,844 \times 20}{110} \qquad\qquad = \underline{41,986}$$

$$\text{NET} = \underline{£419,858}$$

Assuming a 50/50 labour and material ratio then the value of labour will be:

$$£419,858 \times 15\% = \underline{£209,929}$$

If a 45-hour week was worked and an average rate for craftsmen and labourer was £5.50 per hour, then the number of man weeks contained in the final account will be:

$$\frac{£209,929}{£5.50 \times 45 \text{ hours per week}} = 848 \text{ man weeks}$$

The second part of the calculation is to ascertain the quantum of disruption and requires the total number of hours actually worked by the Contractor exclusive of non-productive overtime. This can be obtained from the weekly returns of the clerk of works usually agreed between the Contractor and the clerk of works for those operatives concerned in the contract. All supervision by personnel not actually engaged in the building operations must be omitted, as well as all labour concerned in the preliminaries. This is the subject of the contract period costs and prolongation labour. It will have been observed that the preliminaries were deducted from the amount of the final account, as was the financial value of overtime ordered by the Architect. The question of increased costs will be dealt with shortly and subsequently. It also goes without saying that any of the Contractor's labour used by Named Sub-contractors will also need adjustment, as well as the payment for specific disruption agreed.

If it is found that the total net man weeks actually worked by the Contractor's operatives amounts to 1,317, then the various adjustments and abatements previously discussed now need implementing and are given below:

			Man Weeks
Total of net man weeks			1,317

Less

Labour in preliminaries which will be claimed independently)	= 88	
Labour utilised by Named Sub-contractor	= 29	
Specific disruptions separately paid for	= 54	
Labour in supervision	= 126	
Abatements under clause 4.1	= 32	329
		= 988
Less 2% risk element		= 20
		= 968
Less man weeks contained in the final account as previously calculated		= 848
DIFFERENCE		= 120 Man weeks

However, the Employer is only financially liable for 11 weeks of the 21 weeks over-run or extension of time which reduces the disruption to:

$$\frac{11 \text{ weeks}}{21 \text{ weeks}} \times 120 \text{ man weeks} = 63 \text{ man weeks}$$

The average cost of a 45 hour week is therefore:

45 hours x £5.50   = £248

To this will be added price fluctuations which might be considered to be as a percentage:

$$\frac{£26,667}{461,884} \times 100 = \underline{5.77\%}$$

The value of the average weekly cost will therefore be:

$$£248 + 5.77\%$$

$$= \quad 248 + £14$$

$$= \quad \underline{£262}$$

Since the Employer, subject to agreement by his professional advisers, is liable for 63 man weeks, the value of the claim under clauses 4.7 and 4.11 for direct loss and expense will be:

$$£262 \times 63 \text{ man weeks} = £16,506$$

Finally, the claim of £16,506 receives a 7% addition for recurring overheads as follows:

$$£16,506 + 7\% \text{ overheads}$$

$$= \quad £16,506 + £1,155$$

$$= \quad \underline{£17,661}$$

It cannot be overstressed that each and every link in the contractual claim must be fully capable of being proved to a civil standard of proof. In regard to claims for disruption there is usually a great degree of challenge by the Employer's professional advisers. Therefore, the Contractor must have the material facts ready to hand to achieve a successful negotiation.

APPENDIX: EXAMPLE OF A PROLONGATION CLAIM

IN THE MATTER OF CLAIM NO. 1 BY MESSRS XYZ LTD (CONTRACTORS) AGAINST THE BUILDING EMPLOYER ARISING OUT OF THE EXECUTION OF A CONTRACT AT THE SOUTHERN COAST

January 1991

CONTRACT PARTICULARS

1. Contract sum   = £409,116

2. Final account   = £651,996

3. Contract period   = 52 weeks

4. Actual time   = 73 weeks

5. Total over-run   = 21 weeks

6. Of the 21 weeks and over-run there are 11 weeks with financial liability for the Employer and 10 weeks without financial liability by the Employer.

7. Since there is no unaccounted time there cannot be any deduction of liquidated damages under clause 2.7.

EXTENSION OF TIME CERTIFICATE

Under clauses 2.3 to 2.5 and clause 2.9 formal notification was given by the Contractor requesting applicable extensions of time. After considerable negotiation a certificate for an extension of time was duly granted by the Architect for 21 weeks, of which 11 weeks was held to be at the Employer's financial liability.

Pursuant to clauses 4.7 (last paragraph) and 4.11 claims for reimbursement of direct loss and/or expense were submitted for prolongation. (Disturbance of the regular progress of the works is the subject of a separate, later claim.).

The details and genesis of the claim are based on the previous 'Allocation diagram for an extension of time'.

Agent

The agent only stayed on the contract for six weeks of the over-run which had financial liability for the Employer. (Note clause 3.4.)

Weekly wage	=	£300
Add 50% for pension, bonus, National Insurance, holidays, sickness and redundancy payments	=	£150
		£450
£450 x 6 weeks	=	£2700

Sub-agent

The sub-agent stayed on the contract for the whole of the contract and over-run of which 11 weeks are at the Employer's financial liability. (Note clause 3.4.)

Weekly wage	=	£200
Add 50% for pension, bonus, National Insurance, holidays, sickness and redundancy payments	=	£100
	=	£300
£300 x 11 weeks	=	£3300

Store-keeper and time clerk

The part-time post of store-keeper and part-time clerk are performed by one man. The cost would be for the 11 weeks which are the Employer's liability.

Weekly wage	=	£150
Add 50% for pension, bonus, National Insurance, holidays, sickness and redundancy payments	=	£75
		£225
225 x 11 weeks	=	£2475

Site offices and accommodation, together with furniture and equipment

The cost of the Main Contractor's offices and accommodation (excluding attendance and cleaning) may be based on the plan area per m^2 at a price of £2 per m^2. This is 120 m^2.

100 m^2 x £2 x 11 weeks	=	£2200

Attendance on offices and accommodation

One operative per day of 8 hours for 5 days a week at £6 per hour is

1 x 8 x 5 x £5 x 11 weeks	=	£2640

130

Local authority rates for temporary offices and accommodation
The local authority rates are £35 per week;

£35 x 11 weeks   =   £660

Storage sheds and sanitary accommodation
The cost of storage sheds and sanitary accommodation is £60 per week.

£60 x 11 weeks   =   £60

Attendance on storage sheds and sanitary accommodation
One operative for 4 hours a day and 5 days a week at £6 per hour.

1 x 4 x 5 x £6 x 11 weeks   = £1320

Toilet rolls, soap, towels and disinfectant
The cost of providing the essential toiletries is £15 per week.

£15 x 11 weeks   =   £65

Welfare, canteen equipment and subsidy
The cost of renting the welfare accommodation, canteen, tables, chairs and equipment is £150 per week, in addition to which there is a canteen subsidy of £40 per week.

(150 + £40) x 11 weeks   = £2090

Attendance on safety, first aid, drying clothes and protective clothing
The value of attendance is one operative for 4 hours a day, 5 days a week for 11 weeks.

1 x 4 x 5 x £6 x 11 weeks   = £1320

Provision of first aid materials, drying facilities and protective clothing

First aid dressings, bandages, elastoplast and
medicines, etc.   =   £11

Drying units x 4 x £15   =   £60

Replacement of protective clothing, oil skins, boots,
goggles, gloves and masks etc.   =   £50

Cost per week   =   £121

£121 x 11 weeks   = £1,331

Mechanical plant

The total cost of the mechanical plant is £70,000 and is priced solely in the Preliminaries. A deduction must be made for loading and delivering the plant to site and subsequently loading and delivering back to the plant yard or to any hirers. If this cost is £14,000 then the net cost is £70,000 - £14,000 = £56,000. If £11,000 is recouped through daywork and £24,000 through measured work the value is:

£56,000 - (£11,000 + £24,000)   = £21,000

If the plant is used uniformly over the contract then the weekly cost will be:

$$\frac{£2,000}{(52\text{-}11)} = \frac{£21,000}{63} = £444$$

On the basis that the mechanical plant is required for an extra 11 weeks:

£144 x 11 weeks   = £4,884

Concrete batching plant

The concrete mixer and fuel together with cement silo, weigh batcher and bays for sand and aggregates, costs £300 per week, then the cost for 6 weeks will be:

£300 x 6   = £1,800

It is assumed that the labour for producing and placing the concrete is included in the contract rates.

De-watering water table

Because of the discovery of an unexpected water table during the execution of the foundations and subsequent drainage and external works, additional removal of water below the water table was necessary. The periods involved were 4 weeks for the foundations and 7 weeks for the drainage and external works, making a total of 11 weeks. The cost per week is £170.

£170 x 11   = £1,870

Extended hire period of scaffolding

It was agreed that the scaffolding was needed for an extra 20 weeks. If the total cost of the scaffolding was £53,000 at least £4,000 must be deducted for delivery to site and subsequent removal from site, which equals £53,000 - £4,000 = £49,000.

If the extended hire charge is 25% then the cost will be £49,000 - 75% - £49,000 - 36,750 = £12,250. Since the original period for scaffolding was 26 weeks the cost per week is:

$$\frac{£12,250}{26} = £471 \text{ per week}$$

The extended hire charge for 20 weeks will be:

£471 x 20   = <u>£9,420</u>

Hoist

There were three hoists used in connection with the scaffolding which will have been required for the 20 weeks liability period. The cost of each hoist and attendant labour amounted to £230 per week:

£230 x 3 x 20   = <u>£13,800</u>

Service gang

For a contract of this magnitude at least a service gang of two labourers will be needed. For a day of 10 hours 5 days a week at £6 per hour, the cost will be:

2 x 10 x 5 x £6 x 11   = <u>£6,600</u>

Telephone

The cost of a business line is taken as £2 per week and assuming two lines are necessary and that the cost of calls is £28 per week for both lines, the total cost will be 2 x £2 = £4 plus £28, which is £32 per week.

£32 x 11   = <u>£803</u>

Security

The cost of providing the necessary security to the contract at nights and for weekends is £500 per week:

£500 x 11   = <u>£5,500</u>

Water for the contract

The cost of water has not been adjusted in the final account and it must be dealt with in the prolongation claim. It is a function of time and not one of value.

The cost of water was given in the contract bills as £1,000 when the contract sum was £409,116. Since the final account value is now £651,996 then the revised cost will be:

$$\frac{£1,000 \times £651,996}{£409,116} = \underline{£1,594}$$

But since £1,000 is already in the contract sum only the difference needs to be claimed:

£1,594 - £1,000   = <u>£594</u>

Insurance for the contract

The cost of the contract insurance is £8,000 and has not been adjusted in the final account; it must be evaluated in the prolongation claim. The cost of insurance is both a function of time and value. The period of time concerned is 52 weeks plus 11 weeks over-run at the financial liability of the Employer. This totals 63 weeks in all. The revised cost of insurance will be:

$$£8,000 \times \frac{£651,996}{£409,116} \times \frac{63 \text{ weeks}}{52 \text{ weeks}} = £15,446$$

But since £8,000 is already in the contract sum only the difference needs to be claimed:

$$£15,446 - £8,000 = £7,446$$

Defects liability

The defects liability now extends over 63 weeks and is concerned with £651,996 instead of £409,116. If the estimated value of defects liability is 0.5% the extra cost will be:

$$£651,996 \times (0.5\%) \times \frac{63 \text{ weeks}}{52 \text{ weeks}} = £3,950$$

But the contractual allowance would have been:

$$£409,116 \times (0.5\%) = £2,046$$

The extra value of defects liability is therefore:

$$£3,950 - £2,046 = £1,904$$

TOTAL COST OF PROLONGATION

The total cost of the prolongation claim will be:

1. Agent	2,700
2. Sub-agent	3,300
3. Store-keeper and time clerk	2,475
4. Site offices and accommodation together with furniture and equipment	2,200
5. Attendance on offices	2,640
6. Cleaning materials	55

7. Local authority rates	385
8. Storage sheds and sanitary accommodation	660
9. Attendance on (8)	1,320
10. Materials	65
11. Welfare and canteen	2,090
12. Attendance on (11)	1,320
13. Materials, etc.	1,331
14. Mechanical plant	4,884
15. Concrete batching plant	1,800
16. De-watering	1,870
17. Scaffolding	9,420
18. Hoist	13,800
19. service gang	6,600
20. Telephone	352
21. Electricity	803
22. Security	5,500
23. Water	594
24. Insurance	7,446
25. Defects liability	1,904
TOTAL	= £75,514

Overheads

To the sum of 75,514 the Contractor is entitled to claim for his variable overheads which on a contract of this magnitude is 7%:

Net cost of prolongation   = £75,514

Add 7% variable overheads   = <u>£5,286</u>

                                              <u>£80,800</u>

Contractors are attracted to the theory that they are entitled to a time-related basis for overheads. This is not legally acceptable because of the decision in the House of Lords case of *Tate & Lyle v The Greater London Council* (1983) where this issue was fully explored and rejected.

Commentary on prolongation items

It is not suggested that the list of items is exhaustive since every contract will contain its own specific items of claim. Detailed arguments concerning the various items of a prolongation claim are given on pages 87 - 97 of '*Contractor's claims under JCT80*'.

TABLE OF CASES